Pg. 55

Pg. 121

Pg. 58

A Toronto born mother of four children, Lorraine Hammett was not able to fulfill her lifelong wish to be a school teacher. To satisfy her own need, and the needs of others, she embarked on an exciting career path.

After several years in the world of direct selling, she became a consultant in the fields of self improvement, major appliances, and scarf fashion. Her interest in scarves began in 1971 when she was instrumental in marketing the scarf clip in southern Ontario and major western Canadian cities. As a result of the success of the scarf clip, she recognized the need for further instructions about the magic of scarf fashion.

This book is Lorraine's response to her many customers and friends who admire her ability to *"TIE ONE ON."*

THE KNAUGHTY LOOK™

(THE MAGIC OF SCARF FASHION)

By Lorraine E. Hammett

ISBN 0-9691605-0-X

Mail enquiries to ...

**HAMMETT ENTERPRISES
16 ADA CRESCENT
SCARBOROUGH, ONTARIO, CANADA
M1P 4A8**

•

Cover design by Ross Caldarola
Illustrations by Robert Finnemore
Blood, sweat and tears by my dear husband Tom and family

•

Printed in Canada by Concord Graphics Inc.

A. **TAKE** TWO SCARVES, RIGHT SIDES TOGETHER, AND **STITCH** A HALF INCH (1.2 cm) SEAM AT BOTH SIDES TO FORM THE SIDE SEAMS OF THE SKIRT. **MEASURE** FROM THE WAIST TO FIND THE DESIRED LENGTH. **CUT** EXCESS MATERIAL FROM THE TOP.

B. AT THE TOP EDGE OF THE SKIRT BACK ONLY, **TURN** UNDER A QUARTER INCH (.5 cm) AND **PRESS.** **TURN** UNDER ANOTHER 3/8 INCH (.8 cm) FROM THE PRESSED FOLD AND **PIN-STITCH** TO MAKE A CASING FOR THE ELASTIC.

C. AT THE TOP EDGE OF THE SKIRT FRONT, **SEW** ONE MACHINE GATHERING ROW 5/8 INCH (1.5 cm) FROM THE CUT EDGE. **THEN** SEW ANOTHER ROW ONE QUARTER INCH (.5 cm) FROM THE CUT EDGE.

BODICE:

D. **FOLD** A SCARF IN HALF TO FORM A TRIANGLE. **CUT** ALONG THE FOLD. **SEW** A HEM ON THE CUT EDGE OF ONE HALF AND KEEP IT TO BE USED AS A HEAD COVERING. **PLACE** THE OTHER HALF ON A FLAT SURFACE.

E. **DRAW** A LINE 12 INCHES (30.5 cm) FROM THE CUT EDGE. **CUT** ON THIS NEW LINE. (NOTE, THE LITTLE TRIANGLE IS NOT NEEDED). **FOLD** THE LONG PIECE IN HALF. ON THE SHORT EDGE, MEASURING FROM THE FOLD, **MAKE** A MARK THAT IS A QUARTER OF YOUR WAIST MEASUREMENT PLUS ONE INCH (2.5 cm). **DRAW** A LINE FROM YOUR MARK TO THE POINT AT THE END OF THE LONG EDGE. **CUT** BOTH ENDS OF THE BODICE ON THIS LINE. **UNFOLD** THE PIECE OF SCARF, **TURN** THE CUT EDGES, AND **STITCH** NARROW HEMS.

FINAL STEPS:

F. **PIN** THE WAIST EDGE OF THE BODICE PIECE TO THE FRONT OF THE UPPER EDGE OF THE SKIRT. THE ENDS OF THE BODICE SHOULD MEET THE SIDE SEAMS OF THE SKIRT. **MATCH** UP THE CENTRE FRONTS WITH THE EDGES EVEN AND THE RIGHT SIDES TOGETHER. **GATHER** THE SKIRT FRONT TO FIT THE BODICE, **SPREAD** THE GATHERS EVENLY AND **STITCH** A 5/8 (1.5 cm) SEAM.

G. **MAKE** A HEM AT THE UPPER EDGE OF THE BODICE, **TURNING** IN THE ENDS TO MATCH THE SHAPE OF THE TIP.

H. **TAKE** ELASTIC HALF YOUR WAIST MEASUREMENT AND **INSERT** IT INTO THE SKIRT CASING. **SEW** IT SECURELY AT EACH END.

for those special occasions, we suggest you look at the designs
on pages 6, 13, 16 or 37

INDEX

MATERIALS: THREE 36 INCH (91.5 cm) SQUARE SCARVES.
1/4 INCH (.5 cm) WIDE ELASTIC.
USE A FINE NEEDLE ON THE MACHINE

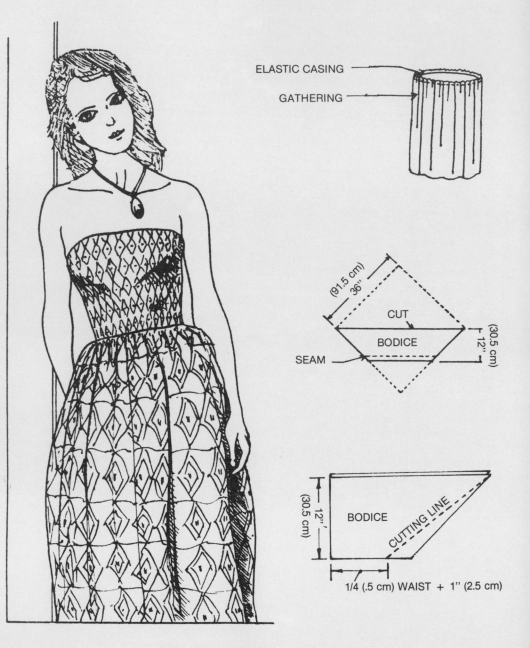

ELASTIC CASING

GATHERING

(91.5 cm)
36"

CUT

(30.5 cm)
12"

BODICE

SEAM

12"
(30.5 cm)

BODICE

CUTTING LINE

1/4 (.5 cm) WAIST + 1" (2.5 cm)

THE KNAUGHTY LOOK

It is true to say that a wardrobe is a reflection of your fashion taste in form, fabric and colour, your degree of acceptance of the 'in-fashion', your clothing budget and your personality. Building a fashion wardrobe with a manageable budget needs the careful selection of your basic garments so that their style, colour and fabric can co-cordinate with each other. The basic items include jackets, coats, skirts, dresses, blouses, sweaters and shirts. With the application of a little imagination (which we are all blessed with), you can create an attractive mix-and-match ensemble that gives you a 'different look' each time you dress. But the change of look doesn't end there because it can be further enhanced and highlighted by the innovative use of your accessories selected from jewellery, belts, gloves, shoes, hosiery and hats. However, there is one accessory that can provide more versatility in look and charm than any other, and it is probably tucked away in your dresser drawer ...... the SCARF.

THE TOUCH OF CLASS

A stylish, adaptable, patterned apparel, the scarf can be created into more delightful modes than any single accessory you possess. A scarf deftly tied, folded, draped, pinned or twisted can add a 'touch of class' to your appearance limited only by your own skill and fancy. "For me," says fashion consultant and demonstrator, Lorraine Hammett, "the scarf is a flattering and versatile fashion accessory. Creatively used, it provides many changes of look to my basic wardrobe and adds exciting dimension of chicness at very modest cost." In selecting a scarf, it is important to blend the scarf's fabric and colours with those of the basic apparel you intend to wear.

The next important step is knowing how to fashion the scarf into one of numerous creative shapes and folds, the one that adds that 'touch of class' to your outfit. Lorraine looks upon the scarf as a highlight accessory that images your emotion, feeling and sexuality for each occasion. In addition it complements and stirs admiration of you and your appearance. Cleverly used, says Lorraine, the scarf can draw attention away from any figure fault and centre eyes on the more attractive aspects of your figure and personality.

MATERIALS: FIVE LONG SCARVES,
              ABOUT 14 BY 60 INCHES (35.5 - 152.4 cm).
              2-1/2 YARDS (228.7 cm) OF 1/2 INCH
                (1.2 cm) BIAS TAPE.
              1 YARD (91.5 cm) OF 1/4 INCH (.5 cm)
              NON CURL ELASTIC.
              16 INCHES (40.7 cm) SEAM BINDING.

FOR THE SKIRT:

A. **CUT** THREE SCARVES IN HALF CROSSWISE.
B. WITH THE CUT EDGES AT THE WAIST, **PIN** THEN **SEW** THE PIECES WITH RIGHT SIDES TOGETHER TO MAKE A SIX PANEL SKIRT.
C. OPEN OUT ONE EDGE OF HALF INCH BIAS TAPE AND **PIN** IT, RIGHT SIDES TOGETHER, TO THE UPPER (CUT) EDGE OF THE SKIRT. **TURN** OVER THE TAPE ENDS, **TRIM** AS NEEDED, AND **STITCH** ALONG THE LONG FOLDED LINE. **TURN** TAPE TO THE INSIDE AND **STITCH** THE OUTER EDGE TO INSIDE OF THE SKIRT TO MAKE A CASING.
D. **CUT** 1/4 INCH (.5 cm) ELASTIC ONE INCH LONGER THAN WAIST SIZE. **INSERT** THE ELASTIC IN THE SKIRT CASING AND **STITCH** THE ENDS TOGETHER.

FOR THE BLOUSE:

E. **TAKE** THE OTHER TWO SCARVES, RIGHT SIDES TOGETHER, AND **SEW** THE CENTRE FRONT AND BACK SEAMS UP 15 INCHES (38 cm) FROM EACH END. THE CENTRE OPENING IS THE NECKLINE.
F. **FOLD** SCARVES CROSSWISE WITH RIGHT SIDES TOGETHER. **SEW** 15 INCHES (38 cm) FROM THE BOTTOM EDGE. THIS FORMS THE ARM HOLES.
G. **TRY** ON THE BLOUSE, WRONG SIDE OUT. **PIN** SHOULDER SEAMS TO FIT, SO THE BOTTOM OF BLOUSE IS 6 INCHES (15.2 cm) BELOW YOUR WAIST. **STITCH** AT THE PIN LINE. **TRIM** SEAM ALLOWANCE TO 3/4 INCH (1.8 cm).
H. **SEW** A GATHERING STITCH ACROSS THE SEAM JUST MADE. **CUT** SEAM BINDING TO DESIRED SHOULDER LENGTH. **GATHER** THE SHOULDER OF BLOUSE TO FIT SEAM BINDING. **PIN** AND THEN **STITCH.**

"THE KNAUGHTY LOOK" ... AN ANSWER TO A NEED

Enjoying a successful career as a professional demonstrator and model in the scarf fashion field, Lorraine Hammett was encouraged by both manufacturers and retailers, as well as countless women in her audiences, to produce a book on the 'how' and 'when' of scarf tieing and scarf fashion techniques. Her response to the need is "The Knaughty Look". The book, using simple line drawings, displays how to tie scarves into known and frequently used creative styles plus some of Lorraine's own creations. "I have seen all too often the wistful look on a woman's face as she watches my demonstrations, knowing full well that by the time she reaches home the 'how to do it' lesson would have been long forgotten. By following the instructions in the book and a bit of practice in front of the dresser mirror, those wistful looks will turn into excited smiles".

THE SCARF IN HISTORY

"Coming onto the field of honour, the handsome knight on his black charger prepared for the jousting match sporting from the crown of his armour helmet the crimson silk scarf of fair Gwendolyn". (The Knights of King Arthur). This vignette of ancient days sees the scarf as a personal, delicate item of favour from the gentle lady to her gallant prince. If one could return to prehistoric times and find Mr. and Mrs. Flintrock you would see that they sometimes wore a fur piece that closely resembled a scarf as it was then defined. The early definition of a scarf described a satchel held by strands of materials and slung over one shoulder. The draping of the body with cloth prevailed for centuries as fashioned by the Greeks and Romans. The Indian 'sari' is a present day example of that kind of dress.

The Assyrians introduced and favoured the SHAWL worn over a tunic. Back in the 3rd and 4th Centuries one would find the origin of the modern day wonderment, the BIKINI. Indeed it was really a scarf discreetly placed and fastened ... What's new ladies?

STOLES appeared in the 10th Century worn by both men and women. In the 14th Century, the scarf as a name passed from describing a satchel to the attractive accessory known today.

The original TURBAN of the 16th Century was described as a 'couvrechef' by the Normans, a 'coverchief' in England and later a headveil. By the 19th Century scarves were fashioned from fine materials for milady's wardrobe. Today, the scarf is as much a stylish fashion item as an accessory for warmth.

By now, you will have perceived that the scarf family is identified with close relatives that include the muffler, ascot, bandana, babushka, boa as well as the above mentioned shawl, stole and turban.

Back to the 20th Century we turn our minds to 'The Knaughty Look'.

A PRETTY DRESS MADE FROM SCARVES.
VERY UNIQUE!   CAN BE WORN AS SHOWN
WITH A BELT OR TRY TUCKING THE
BLOUSE INSIDE THE SKIRT WITH A
MATCHING SCARF OR BELT AROUND
THE WAIST.

ELASTIC CASING

30"

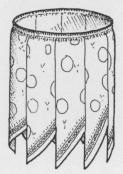

FOR A HANDKERCHIEF HEM
USE BIAS OBLONG SCARVES.

121

CHOOSING SCARVES FOR THE "KNAUGHTY LOOK"

When exploring the spectrum of scarves on a counter top or scanning the display in the show case, several facts as to quality and size of scarves should be kept in mind.

To begin, scarves come in two basic shapes.

Squares:
Medium to large squares are the most versatile size and are ideal for coats providing a fullness and warmth not generally found in oblong styles.   They are also suitable as suit and blouse fillers or as a substitute for a blouse.   When folded they can take on an oblong shape.   Small squares are accent pieces only, very attractive for sport and casual wear.

Small square scarves measure less than 24 inches (60cm).
Medium are 24 to 27 inches (60 to 70 cm).
Large square scarves are 30 inches (75cm) or more.

Oblongs:
Oblong scarves are usually considered an accent item.   With the exception of wool scarves, they are not particularly designed for warmth.   One particular scarf, the bias oblong with its tapered ends, offers a slendering effect and added versatility.   The bias oblong has its own design flair and like the regular oblong is a complementary accessory for suits, dresses, blouses and sweaters.

For oblong scarves, a medium size would be approximately 11 by 54 inches or 27 by 140 cm.   The size and/or proportion of oblong scarves vary.

Again, two general categories identify scarf materials.

Natural: silks, wools and cottons
The dressy silk scarf folds and drapes exceptionally well, ties easily and provides a warmth factor.   Wool scarves offer the greatest warmth and are suitable for sport and casual wear.   The economical cotton scarf is mainly for neck and head covering.

Synthetics: polyesters, acrylics and rayons
Generally less expensive than silk, synthetics can give the classy touch.   They are both versatile and durable.

A chiffon style scarf, whether synthetic or natural fibre, is a delicate, gossamer fabric especially complementary for evening wear.   Its clinging property is very suitable for wearing with a fur coat or as a stylish head cover.

TWIST AN OBLONG
SCARF IN THE
CENTRE, THEN
PLACE THE TWISTED
SCARF AROUND YOUR
BUST AND
TIE A SQUARE KNOT
AT THE BACK.

FOLD A LARGE
SQUARE SCARF INTO
A TRIANGLE AND
PLACE IT AROUND
YOUR HIPS.
TIE A LARGE
SQUARE KNOT AT
THE SIDE.

F U N   I N   T H E   S U N :

HANDLE WITH GENTLE CARE:

When cleaning or washing a scarf follow the manufacturer's instructions. If they are not provided then the following general rules should be applied.

- Acrylic materials can be hand washed.
- Polyester scarves can be hand or machine washed. If using your washer, do so with cool water on the gentle cycle. Drip dry and iron with a low heat setting.
- Silks should be dry cleaned. However, with the greatest of care, silk can be hand washed in cool water and ironed with a very low heat. Test for colour fastness.
- Wool can be dry cleaned, or hand washed in cool water, rolled dry in a towel and ironed at a low heat setting.
- Cleaning the scarf before it becomes too soiled will extend its life. Synthetic fabrics tend to hold stains unless they are treated quickly.
- Careful storing of your scarves makes finding the right one for your ensemble easier. You may prefer to fold and lay them randomly in a drawer. However, by storing according to size and colour, your selection is made easier. Try hanging them according to size and colour.

IDEAS AND REFLECTIONS IN SELECTING:

- Give yourself plenty of time when selecting a scarf. You will be happier with your decisions when you give your imagination and creative ability time to work.
- Wear or bring along some sample of the basic garment. It makes your style and colour choice much easier.
- If possible try on the scarf facing a mirror. Look for its suitability and blend with your features, skin colour and tone.
- Select pattern compatible to pattern. Consider contrast. Stripe designs in a scarf may clash with a stripe design in the basic apparel.
- Keep versatility in mind when making your selection. Can the scarf be used with more than one outfit combination in your wardrobe?
- Choose the size according to how you intend to use the scarf. Is it a major accessory or a simple accent piece? Will it be worn on the head, the neck, or around the waist?
- Everyone has certain colours they like and dislike. With few exceptions, most of us can wear a broad range of colours.
- Experiment with colour. Although you may not often change your basic colour scheme, blending a colour of your basic garment with a colour in your scarf can result in a delightful addition to your appearance.
- Select good quality scarves. Generally, better quality scarves have straight edges, that is, the edges will parallel exactly when the scarf is folded in half. Look for a rolled edge that is well topstitched.
- Careful consideration of the shape and colours of your scarves can help to minimize a figure problem.

4

FOR A DIFFERENT SKIRT IDEA:

PLACE THE PAREO AROUND YOUR WAIST OR HIP WITH THE TWO ENDS ON THE LEFT SIDE.

INSTEAD OF TYING THE TWO CORNERS TOGETHER, **HOLD** THEM IN YOUR RIGHT HAND AND **MOVE** YOUR LEFT HAND BACK ALONG THE EDGE FOR TEN TO TWELVE INCHES (25.5 - 30.5 cm) AND **FORM** A POINT.

NOW **TIE** THE POINT AND THE RIGHT CORNER IN A KNOT.

TUCK THE LOOSE CORNER UP AND OVER THE KNOT FOR A FINISHED EFFECT.

FOR THE TOP:

TIE A LOOSE KNOT IN THE MIDDLE OF AN OBLONG SCARF.

PLACE THE KNOTTED SCARF AROUND YOUR BUST AND

TIE A SQUARE KNOT AT THE BACK.

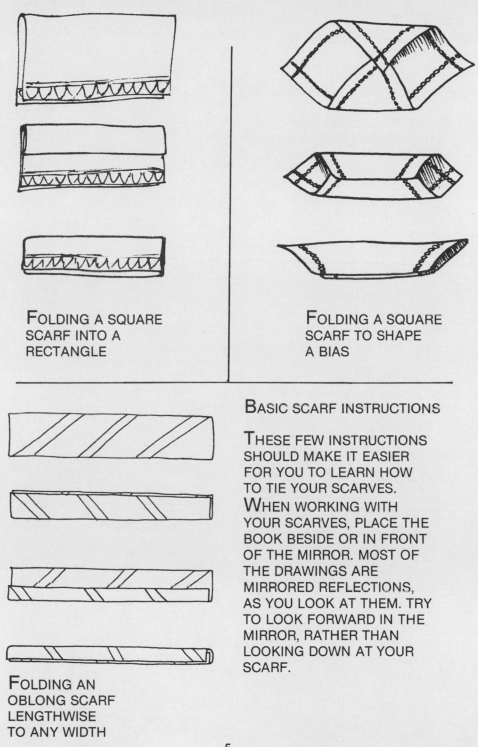

FOLDING A SQUARE
SCARF INTO A
RECTANGLE

FOLDING A SQUARE
SCARF TO SHAPE
A BIAS

BASIC SCARF INSTRUCTIONS

THESE FEW INSTRUCTIONS
SHOULD MAKE IT EASIER
FOR YOU TO LEARN HOW
TO TIE YOUR SCARVES.
WHEN WORKING WITH
YOUR SCARVES, PLACE THE
BOOK BESIDE OR IN FRONT
OF THE MIRROR. MOST OF
THE DRAWINGS ARE
MIRRORED REFLECTIONS,
AS YOU LOOK AT THEM. TRY
TO LOOK FORWARD IN THE
MIRROR, RATHER THAN
LOOKING DOWN AT YOUR
SCARF.

FOLDING AN
OBLONG SCARF
LENGTHWISE
TO ANY WIDTH

FOLD A LARGE SQUARE INTO A TRIANGLE.
PLACE THE FOLDED SCARF DIAGONALLY ACROSS YOUR CHEST.
TAKE ONE END UNDER ONE ARM AND THE OTHER END OVER YOUR OPPOSITE SHOULDER.
CROSS THE ENDS UNDER YOUR ARM AND
TIE ON TOP OF YOUR SHOULDER.

TO MAKE THE SKIRT, JUST
WRAP THE PAREO AROUND YOUR WAIST OR HIPS AND
TIE A SQUARE KNOT WITH THE ENDS.

A SIMPLE VARIATION FOR THE BODICE.
FOLD A LARGE SQUARE INTO A TRIANGLE. **PLACE** THE FOLDED EDGE ACROSS YOUR CHEST AND **TIE** A SQUARE KNOT AT THE BACK. IF YOUR LIKE, YOU CAN TUCK THE TRIANGLE INTO THE TOP OF YOUR PAREO.

TAKE A LARGE SQUARE SCARF AND **FOLD** IT INTO A BIAS UNTIL IT IS ABOUT FOUR INCHES WIDE.

TWIST THE SCARF INTO A ROPE.

PLACE THE TWISTED SCARF

ON YOUR FOREHEAD AND **TIE**

A KNOT AT THE BACK.

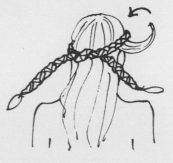

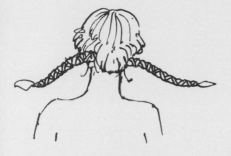

SECTION YOUR HAIR AND

TUCK IT INTO THE TWISTED SCARF.

BRING THE ENDS TO THE FRONT

AND **TIE**. IF THEY'RE NOT

LONG ENOUGH TO TIE, SIMPLY

TUCK THEM IN.

IN THE 'SUN SEASON' USE YOUR GIANT SCARF AS A BODY
WRAP FOR A SUN DRESS OR A BATHING SUIT COVER-UP.

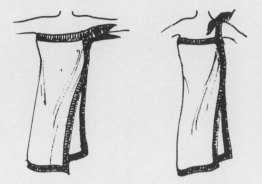

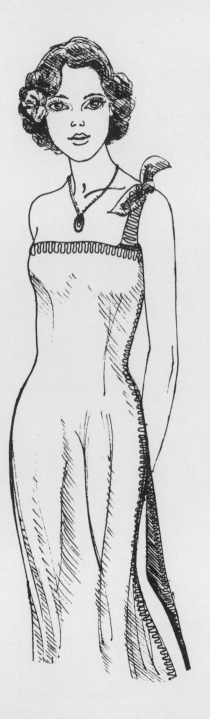

PLACE THE PAREO ACROSS
YOUR CHEST.

TAKE THE ENDS UNDER
ONE ARM.

TWIST THE ENDS AND BRING
THEM UP OVER YOUR
SHOULDER.

TIE A SQUARE KNOT.

A PAREO CAN BE MADE FROM A

VERY LARGE SQUARE SCARF,

50 TO 60 INCHES (127 - 152.4 cm)

SQUARE.

TAKE A LARGE SQUARE SCARF AND
FOLD IT INTO A TRIANGLE.

PLACE THE FOLDED EDGE ON YOUR
FOREHEAD AND **TWIST** THE
ENDS INTO A ROPE.

TAKE THE TWISTED ENDS TO THE BACK
OF YOUR HEAD AND **TIE** A
SECURE KNOT.

TAKE A SECOND SCARF AND **TWIST** IT INTO A ROPE.

PLACE IT AROUND YOUR
HEAD AND **TIE** A KNOT
AT THE BACK.

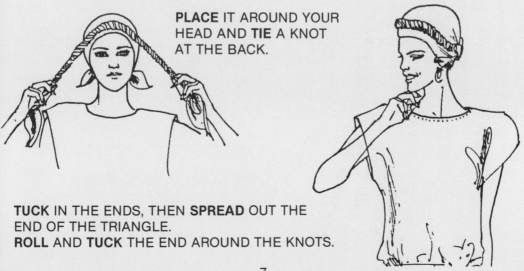

TUCK IN THE ENDS, THEN **SPREAD** OUT THE
END OF THE TRIANGLE.
ROLL AND **TUCK** THE END AROUND THE KNOTS.

TWIST A SMALL SQUARE SCARF TO FORM A ROPE. **WRAP** IT AROUND THE CROWN AND **TIE** A SQUARE KNOT.

SPREAD THE ENDS.

TAKE AN OBLONG OR A MEDIUM SQUARE SCARF AND **PLEAT** IT UNTIL IT IS ABOUT 3 INCHES (7.5 cm) WIDE. **PLACE** IT AROUND THE CROWN AND **TIE** A SQUARE KNOT OR **PIN** IN PLACE.

PLEAT A MEDIUM SQUARE SCARF WITH YOUR FINGERS AS SHOWN ON PAGE 83. **WRAP** THE PLEATED SCARF AROUND THE HAT.

FEED THE PLEATED ENDS **DOWN** THROUGH THE LOOP OF THE SCARF CLIP. **SPREAD** THE RUFFLE AND **CLOSE** THE CLIP.

WRAP A BIAS SCARF AROUND THE CROWN AND **MAKE** A BOW USING THE SCARF CLIP AS SHOWN ON PAGE 107.

TAKE A LARGE SQUARE SCARF AND

FOLD IT IN HALF INTO A

RECTANGLE.

PLACE THE FOLDED EDGE ON

YOUR FOREHEAD AND **TAKE** THE

SIDE PANELS TO THE BACK.

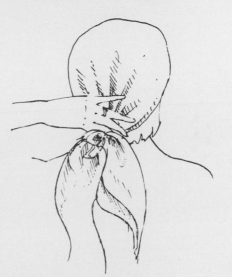

GATHER THE SCARF TOGETHER

AND **HOLD** IT ALL IN

ONE HAND.

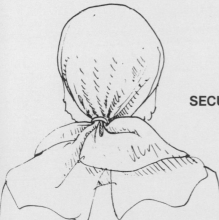

SECURE THE GATHERED SCARF WITH

A PONY TAIL HAIR CLIP. CHOOSE

A DECORATIVE ONE.

PLACE YOUR FAVOURITE

HAT ON TOP TO FINISH

THE LOOK.

USE YOUR SCARF CLIP AS A LOVELY
PIECE OF JEWELLERY. **PLACE** A
SAFETY PIN ON THE INSIDE OF YOUR
SWEATER OR DRESS. **PASS** THE
LOOP OF YOUR SCARF CLIP THROUGH
THE BAR CREATED BY THE SAFETY
PIN. **CLOSE** THE SCARF CLIP.

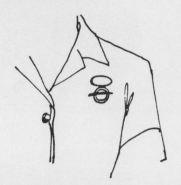

CLIP A SCARF CLIP ON A
CHAIN TO FORM A PENDANT.

CLIP MATCHING SCARF CLIPS
ON A PLAIN PAIR OF SHOES.

PLACE A LARGE SQUARE SCARF
    ON A FLAT SURFACE.

PICK UP THE TWO CORNERS OF
    A STRAIGHT EDGE.

TAKE THE CORNERS TO THE TOP OF
    YOUR HEAD WITH THE
    STRAIGHT EDGE UNDER YOUR CHIN.

TIE A SQUARE KNOT ON THE
CROWN OF YOUR HEAD.

BRING THE SIDE PANELS OF THE
    SCARF TO THE BACK OF YOUR
    HEAD, LAYING ONE PANEL ON
    TOP OF THE OTHER.
TUCK THE SCARF AROUND YOUR
    NECK SECURELY TO GIVE
    A SMOOTH EFFECT.

TAKE YOUR FAVOURITE HAT AND **PLACE**
    IT SECURELY OVER THE SCARF.

RAISE THE COLLAR OF YOUR COAT FOR
    A FINISHED EFFECT.

WONDERFUL FOR POOR WEATHER CONDITIONS.

ANOTHER DESIGN TO TRY WITH THE ATTACHED SCARF.

WRAP THE PANELS AROUND YOUR NECK CRISS-CROSSING THEM AT THE BACK.

THIS SHAPES A TURTLENECK LOOK.

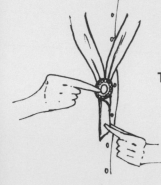

TAKE THE ENDS OF THE SCARF **DOWN** THROUGH THE LOOP OF YOUR SCARF CLIP.

SLIDE THE CLIP UP TO YOUR NECK AND **CLOSE** THE CLIP.

VARIATION: **OPEN** THE SCARF CLIP AND **SWING** ONE PANEL TO YOUR SHOULDER. LET ONE PANEL FALL TO THE BACK AND ONE TO THE FRONT. **CLOSE** THE CLIP AGAIN.

PLACE A SQUARE SCARF ON A FLAT SURFACE.

FOLD IT IN HALF.

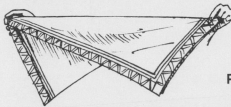

PICK UP THE OPPOSITE CORNERS.

PLACE THE FOLDED EDGE ON YOUR HEAD.

TAKE THE TWO ENDS TO THE BACK AND **TIE** A SQUARE KNOT.

SUGGESTED USES: SHOPPING, GARDENING, CLEANING, ETC.

A CONTINUATION OF OUR BLOUSE WITH TIE SUGGESTIONS.

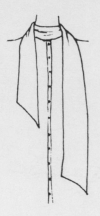

FOR THIS DESIGN, YOU NEED TO

WRAP ONLY ONE PANEL AROUND YOUR NECK.

TAKE THE SHORT END **DOWN** THROUGH THE
    LOOP OF YOUR SCARF CLIP.
PULL THAT PANEL TO ONE SIDE OF THE
    CLIP LOOP MAKING ROOM FOR THE
    OTHER PANEL. **HANG** ON TO THE
    TOP OF THE CLIP.
PINCH THE LONGER PANEL HALF WAY DOWN.
FEED THE PINCH **DOWN** THROUGH THE LOOP
    FORMING A HALF BOW.

ADJUST THE BOW TO YOUR LIKING.

CLOSE THE CLIP.

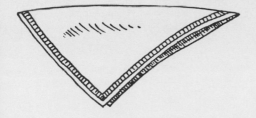

FOLD A LARGE SQUARE SCARF
INTO A TRIANGLE.

TIE A 'RABBIT EAR' KNOT IN
THE POINT OF THE TRIANGLE.

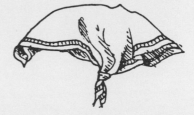

TURN THE KNOT UNDER.

PLACE THE KNOTTED EDGE OF YOUR SCARF
ON THE FRONT OF YOUR HEAD.

BRING THE TWO ENDS TO THE BACK OF
YOUR HEAD AND **TIE**
A SQUARE KNOT.

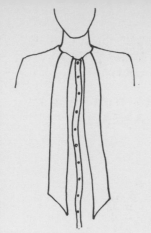

FOR YOUR BLOUSE THAT HAS A SCARF OR TIE ATTACHED ...

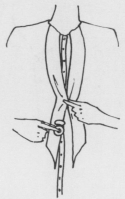

TAKE THE CENTRE EDGES ABOUT FIVE INCHES (12.7 cm) BELOW YOUR NECK AND 'PINCH' THEM TOGETHER.

SEND THE PINCHED EDGES **DOWN** THROUGH THE LOOP OF YOUR SCARF CLIP.

SEPARATE AND **SPREAD** EACH FOLD TO FORM A BOW.

CLOSE THE SCARF CLIP.

112

PLACE THE STRAIGHT EDGE OF A LARGE
SQUARE AT THE BACK OF YOUR
HEAD **UNDER** YOUR HAIR.

BRING THE TWO ENDS OF THAT EDGE TO
THE TOP OF YOUR HEAD,
TIE A SQUARE KNOT.

NOW **TAKE** THE OTHER TWO ENDS AND **TIE**
A LARGE SQUARE KNOT AT THE BACK
OF YOUR HEAD.

YOU NOW HAVE AN ATTRACTIVE COVER-UP

FOR A WINDY DAY.

LAY AN OBLONG SCARF OUT ON A
FLAT SURFACE.
STARTING ABOUT 10 OR 12 INCHES (25.5
- 30.5 cm) FROM ONE END, **PLEAT** OR
GATHER THE SCARF TO 10 OR 12
INCHES (25.5 - 30.5 cm) FROM THE
OTHER END.

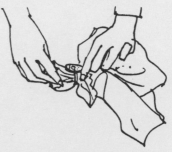

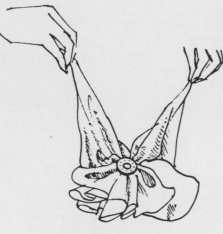

HOLD THE PLEATS WITH ONE HAND,
SEND ONE END OF THE PLEATS **DOWN**
THROUGH THE LOOP OF YOUR
SCARF CLIP.

PUSH THE CLIP TO THE CENTRE OF
THE SCARF AND **CLOSE** THE CLIP.
ARRANGE THE RUFFLE TO YOUR LIKING.
PICK UP THE TWO LONGEST ENDS AND
TIE THEM AROUND YOUR NECK.

ESPECIALLY NICE
USING A SCARF WITH
AN ATTRACTIVE
BORDER.

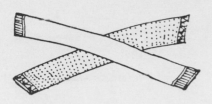

FOLD TWO OBLONG SCARVES IN HALF LENGTHWISE. **PLACE** ONE ON TOP OF THE OTHER TO FORM A CROSS.

LIFT THE BOTTOM SCARF BY THE ENDS TO FORM A LINK.

PLACE THE LINK ON TOP OF YOUR HEAD, **TAKE** THE ENDS TO THE BACK AND **TIE** THEM TOGETHER. **TUCK** IN THE ENDS ON EACH SIDE.

ADD A CLUSTER OF FLOWERS FOR ADDED INTEREST.

TAKE TWO OBLONG SCARVES AND **KNOT** THEM TOGETHER AT ONE END. **TWIST** THEM TIGHTLY AND THEN **KNOT** THE OTHER END.

WRAP AROUND YOUR HEAD AND **TIE** AT THE BACK OF YOUR NECK.

USE HAIRPINS TO HOLD IN PLACE.

TRY USING A FISHNET OR STRETCHY FABRIC.

PLACE AN OBLONG SCARF
AROUND YOUR NECK.

KEEPING BOTH ENDS
EVEN, **OVERLAP** ONE
PANEL ON TOP OF
THE OTHER.

PLACE YOUR THUMB IN
BEHIND THE CENTRE
OF BOTH PANELS AND
PUSH THE SCARF **DOWN**
THROUGH THE LOOP OF
THE SCARF CLIP ABOUT
3 OR 4 INCHES (7.5 - 10.2 cm).

WITH FINGERTIPS ON
THE PUFF, **WORK** THE
SCARF THROUGH THE
CLIP TO MAKE THE
PUFF A LITTLE LARGER.

YOU CAN WEAR THIS

DESIGN IN FRONT AS

A FILLER, OR IT IS

NICE WORN OFF TO

THE SIDE.

TAKE AN OBLONG SCARF.

PLACE THE SCARF ON YOUR HEAD AND **TAKE** THE ENDS TO THE BACK OF YOUR NECK.

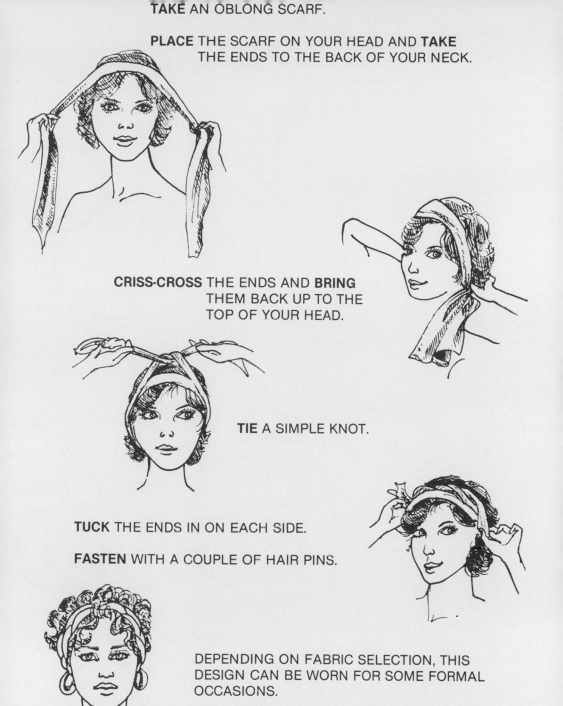

CRISS-CROSS THE ENDS AND **BRING** THEM BACK UP TO THE TOP OF YOUR HEAD.

TIE A SIMPLE KNOT.

TUCK THE ENDS IN ON EACH SIDE.

FASTEN WITH A COUPLE OF HAIR PINS.

DEPENDING ON FABRIC SELECTION, THIS DESIGN CAN BE WORN FOR SOME FORMAL OCCASIONS.

STRETCHY OR SCARVES WITH METALLIC THREADS ARE VERY EFFECTIVE.

FOR A FULLER LOOK, **PLACE** YOUR
FOLDED OBLONG SCARF AT THE FRONT OF
YOUR NECK THEN CRISS-CROSS AT THE BACK,
BRING THE ENDS TO THE FRONT AGAIN.

THEN FOLLOW THE INSTRUCTIONS ON THE
PREVIOUS PAGE.

PLACE AN OBLONG SCARF AROUND
THE BACK OF YOUR HEAD.
BRING THE ENDS FORWARD OVER
YOUR HEAD AND **TWIST** THE ENDS
TWICE.

TAKE THE ENDS TO THE
BACK AGAIN AND **TUCK**
THEM IN OR **TIE** A KNOT.

ALSO WORKS WELL WITH A
SQUARE SCARF FOLDED
INTO A BIAS.

INSTEAD OF TWISTING THE
ENDS, **TIE** A SMOOTH SQUARE
KNOT. THEN **TUCK** THE ENDS
IN NEATLY.

15

TAKE A LARGE OBLONG SCARF AND FOLD IT IN HALF LENGTHWISE.

PLACE THE FOLDED EDGE AROUND YOUR NECK, MAKE THE ENDS EVEN.

PINCH THE FOLDED EDGES TOGETHER ABOUT SEVEN INCHES (17.7 cm) ABOVE THE BOTTOM AND **PUSH** THE PINCH **DOWN** THROUGH THE LOOP OF THE CLIP.

SEPARATE THE FOLDS, WITH THE THUMB AND INDEX FINGER OF EACH HAND, **PULL** ON THE TOP EDGE OF THE FOLD.   THE CLIP WILL MOVE UP THE SCARF BY ITSELF!
WORK THE EDGES TO FORM AN ATTRACTIVE BOW.

WEAR THIS DESIGN UNDER A SUIT JACKET IN PLACE OF A BLOUSE.

PLACE AN OBLONG SCARF AROUND YOUR HEAD.

TAKE ONE PANEL BEHIND YOUR HEAD.

TIE A KNOT AT YOUR EAR.

USING TWO FINGERS AS A
GUIDE **TWIST** ONE PANEL
INTO A ROPE AND
WIND IT AROUND THE KNOT.

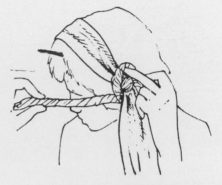

TWIST THE OTHER PANEL
INTO A ROPE AND
ALSO **WIND** IT
AROUND THE KNOT.

SECURE THE KNOT WITH A
HAIRPIN.

TO ACHIEVE A FULL HEAD
COVERING, USE A STRETCHY
SCARF. SEPARATE THE
FOLDS AND BRING TO THE
KNOT. TUCK INTO
THE KNOT AND SECURE
WITH HAIRPINS.

16

TAKE AN OBLONG SCARF AND **PLACE** IT

AROUND YOUR NECK, KEEP THE ENDS EVEN.

OPEN YOUR SCARF CLIP.
PINCH ONE OF THE PANELS
ABOUT HALF WAY DOWN AND
FEED IT **DOWN** THROUGH THE
LOOP OF YOUR CLIP. HANG
ON TO THE TOP OF YOUR CLIP.
REPEAT WITH THE OTHER
PANEL.

USING YOUR THUMBS AND INDEX
FINGERS, **WORK** THE PINCHES
THROUGH THE CLIP LOOP UNTIL
THE OUTER EDGES OF THE SCARF
PASS THROUGH.

CLOSE THE CLIP.

FLUFF THE BOW.

FOR MORE INTEREST, TRY ADDING AN ARTIFICIAL FLOWER
OR A SMALL CLUSTER OF FEATHERS OR ARTIFICIAL FRUIT
TO YOUR SCARF DESIGN.   USE A SMALL OBLONG OR A
SMALL SQUARE SCARF FOLDED INTO THE BIAS.

FEED A PIPECLEANER THROUGH THE PIN
FASTENER OF YOUR ACCENT.

WRAP THE
PIPECLEANER TIGHTLY AROUND
YOUR SCARF.

PLACE THE SCARF AROUND YOUR NECK
AND **TIE** A SQUARE KNOT.
TUCK IN THE SCARF ENDS.

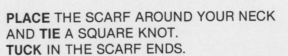

FOR ANOTHER LOOK,
PLACE THE SCARF AROUND YOUR HEAD
AND **TIE** A SQUARE KNOT AT THE SIDE
OR AT THE BACK OF YOUR NECK.

IF YOU WERE TO PIN A FLOWER RIGHT TO YOUR SCARF,
YOU MIGHT DAMAGE THE SCARF.   BY USING OUR
PIPECLEANER SUGGESTION, YOU AVOID THAT POSSIBILITY.

PLACE A SAFETY PIN IN THE UNDERSIDE OF YOUR BLOUSE
OR SWEATER CREATING A BAR FOR YOUR SCARF

PLACE AN OBLONG SCARF AROUND YOUR NECK,
KEEPING ONE SIDE LONGER.

TAKE THE SHORT END **DOWN** THROUGH THE LOOP
OF THE SCARF CLIP.

PULL THE SCARF TO ONE SIDE OF THE LOOP
MAKING ROOM FOR THE OTHER PANEL.

PINCH THE EDGE OF THE LONGER PANEL HALF
WAY DOWN.

FEED THE 'PINCH' **DOWN**
THROUGH THE LOOP
FORMING A HALF BOW.

CLOSE THE CLIP.

SWING THE DESIGN TO YOUR SHOULDER AND
FEED THE END OF THE SCARF INTO THE
SAFETY PIN BAR.

THIS DESIGN WILL STAY IN PLACE NICELY
WITHOUT DAMAGING YOUR SCARVES.

FOLD A SMALL SQUARE SCARF ON THE
BIAS TO ABOUT THREE INCHES WIDE.

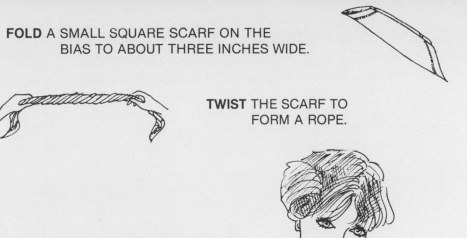

TWIST THE SCARF TO
FORM A ROPE.

PLACE AROUND YOUR NECK AND TIE
A SQUARE KNOT.

VARIATION:

FOR A CHOKER EFFECT, USE A MEDIUM SQUARE
SCARF AND WRAP IT AROUND YOUR NECK TWICE.

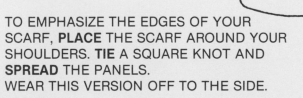

VARIATION:

TO EMPHASIZE THE EDGES OF YOUR
SCARF, **PLACE** THE SCARF AROUND YOUR
SHOULDERS. **TIE** A SQUARE KNOT AND
SPREAD THE PANELS.
WEAR THIS VERSION OFF TO THE SIDE.

TAKE AN OBLONG SCARF AND FOLD IT IN THIRDS LENGTHWISE UNTIL IT IS ABOUT FIVE INCHES (12.7 cm) WIDE.

PLACE IN FRONT OF YOUR NECK.
TAKE THE ENDS TO THE BACK OF YOUR NECK.
CRISS-CROSS THE PANELS AND BRING THEM FORWARD TO THE FRONT.

TAKE THE ENDS OF THE SCARF **DOWN** THROUGH THE LOOP OF THE SCARF CLIP.

SLIDE THE CLIP UP THE SCARF TO THE NECK, THEN LET GO OF THE CLIP.
SWING ONE PANEL TO THE SHOULDER FOR A SIDE EFFECT.
CLOSE THE CLIP.

GIVES THE ILLUSION OF HEIGHT.

FOLD A SMALL SQUARE SCARF ON THE
BIAS TO ABOUT THREE INCHES (7.5 cm) WIDE.

TAKE A PEARL OR BEAD NECKLACE SHORTER THAN
THE LENGTH OF THE SCARF.

TWIST THE NECKLACE AROUND THE SCARF
AND **PLACE** AROUND YOUR NECK.

CLOSE THE CLASP OF
THE NECKLACE.

TIE A SQUARE KNOT DIRECTLY
OVER THE CLASP.

FOR EVENING WEAR.

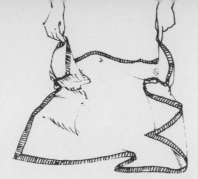

PLACE A LARGE SQUARE SCARF ON A

FLAT SURFACE.

PICK UP TWO CORNERS OF A STRAIGHT

EDGE WITH YOUR FINGERS.

BEGIN TO **TWIST** THE SCARF IN

ONE DIRECTION, KEEPING

THE TWISTS FAIRLY LOOSE.

CAREFULLY **PICK** UP THE TWISTED SCARF

AND **PLACE** AROUND YOUR NECK.

WITH ONE HAND HOLDING THE ENDS,

SEND THE ENDS **DOWN** THROUGH THE LOOP

OF YOUR SCARF CLIP.

SLIDE THE CLIP UP TO DESIRED

LENGTH AND **CLOSE.**

FLUFF AND ARRANGE

THE SCARF.

OPEN A SQUARE SCARF AND PLACE IT ON A FLAT SURFACE.

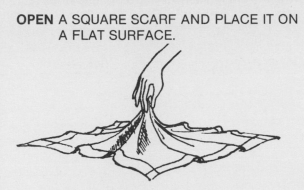

PICK UP THE CENTRE OF THE SCARF AND **TIE** A SIMPLE OVERHAND OR 'RABBIT EAR' KNOT.

TAKE OPPOSITE CORNERS OF THE SCARF AND FORM A TRIANGLE WITH THE KNOT HIDDEN ON THE INSIDE.

PLACE THE SCARF AROUND YOUR NECK WITH THE KNOT UNDER YOUR CHIN. **BRING** THEM FORWARD UNDER THE PANEL. **TIE** A SQUARE KNOT.

IF THE SCARF IS SMALL, TIE THE KNOT AT THE BACK AND TUCK IN ENDS.

HERE'S AN EXCITING VARIATION FOR THE DESIGN

ON THE PRECEDING PAGE! **PLACE** THE CLIP AT

THE BACK AND **FLUFF** THE TRIANGLE AT THE FRONT.

LOOKS GREAT WITH TURTLE NECK SWEATERS.

FOR A VARIATION ON THE PRECEDING

DESIGN, AFTER TIEING THE

KNOT IN THE CENTRE OF YOUR SCARF,

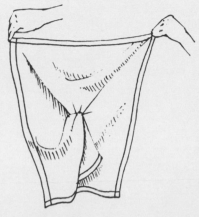

PICK UP TWO CORNERS OF A STRAIGHT EDGE.

PLACE THE SCARF AROUND YOUR NECK.

CRISS-CROSS THE ENDS, THEN **BRING** THEM FORWARD UNDER THE CHIN.

TIE A SQUARE KNOT.

ANOTHER GOOD FILLER FOR YOUR BLOUSES AND JACKETS.

FOLD A SQUARE SCARF INTO A TRIANGLE AND **PLACE** IT AROUND YOUR NECK, FOLDED EDGE NEXT TO YOUR NECK.

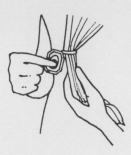

FEED THE ENDS **DOWN** THROUGH THE LOOP OF YOUR OPEN FACED SCARF CLIP.

SLIDE THE CLIP UP THE SCARF ABOUT SIX OR SEVEN INCHES. **SPREAD** EACH PANEL SEPARATELY, ONE ON TOP OF THE OTHER.

TAKE THE TIPS OF THE PANELS BACK UP THROUGH THE NECK OPENING AND **DOWN** THROUGH THE OPEN FACE OF YOUR SCARF CLIP.

SPREAD AND SEPARATE THE PANELS AGAIN AND **CLOSE** THE CLIP.

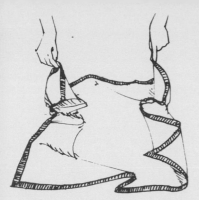

AFTER **PLACING** A LARGE SQUARE
SCARF ON A FLAT SURFACE,
PICK UP TWO CORNERS OF A
STRAIGHT EDGE WITH YOUR
FINGERS.

TWIST THE SCARF IN ONE DIRECTION. BE SURE
THE FIRST TWIST GOES TO THE CENTRE OF
THE SCARF. **TWIST** SEVERAL TIMES, KEEPING
THE TWISTS FAIRLY LOOSE.

REPEAT WITH THE OTHER TWO ENDS.
CAREFULLY **PICK** UP THE TWISTED
SCARF AND **PLACE** IT AROUND YOUR
NECK.

TAKE THE TWO ENDS AND
TIE A SQUARE KNOT.

FLUFF AND ARRANGE THE
SCARF TO YOUR LIKING.

FOLD A SQUARE SCARF INTO A TRIANGLE AND **PLACE** IT AROUND YOUR SHOULDERS.

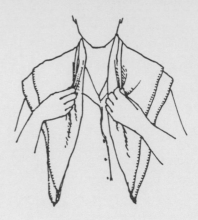

PICK UP THE CENTRE OF EACH TOP LAYER AND **PINCH** THE EDGES TOGETHER.

SEND THE PINCHED EDGES **DOWN** THROUGH THE LOOP OF YOUR SCARF CLIP.

SLIDE THE CLIP UP ABOUT THREE INCHES (7.5 cm).
SEPARATE THE PINCHED EDGES.

FLUFF EACH BOW FROM THE BACK OF THE SCARF WITH YOUR FINGERTIPS.

CLOSE THE SCARF CLIP.

101

TAKE A LARGE SQUARE SCARF.

FOLD IN HALF INTO A RECTANGLE. CONTINUE FOLDING
IN HALF UNTIL THE SCARF IS ABOUT THREE INCHES (7.5 cm) WIDE.

PLACE AROUND YOUR NECK AND **TIE** A
SINGLE, SIMPLE OVERHAND KNOT.

FOR ONE VARIATION:

TO GET THE BOW TIE LOOK, FOLLOW
THE STEPS ABOVE, THEN ...

TIE A SECOND KNOT FORMING THE
SQUARE KNOT.

FOR ANOTHER VARIATION:

BUILD YOURSELF A FLOWER BY COMPLETING
THE BOW TIE AND ...

BEND THE STITCHED EDGE BACKWARDS.

A FLORAL VARIATION OF THE CHIC BOW USING A SCARF CLIP
WITH AN OPEN FACE.

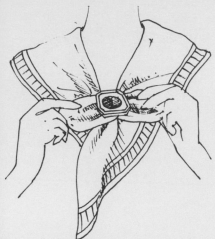

AFTER COMPLETING THE DESIGN ON THE PRECEDING PAGE, **OPEN** THE CLIP. **MAKE** THE BOW AS BIG AS POSSIBLE WITHOUT LOSING THE ENDS OF YOUR SCARF.

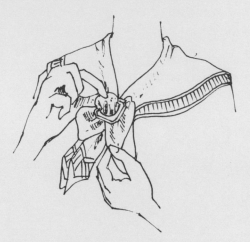

TAKE THE UPPER FOLDED EDGES OF THE BOW AND **FEED** THEM **UP** THROUGH THE OPEN FACE OF YOUR CLIP.

AS YOU CONTINUE TO **PULL** THE EDGES THROUGH, YOU WILL SEE THAT YOU ARE FORMING FOUR PETALS.

WHEN THE PETALS ARE BALANCED, **CLOSE** THE CLIP.

SPREAD AND FLATTEN THE PETALS.

WEAR OFF TO ONE SIDE
     FOR A FLATTERING EFFECT.

FOLD A SQUARE SCARF INTO A TRIANGLE.

PLACE THE FOLDED EDGE OVER YOUR
    NOSE.
TAKE THE ENDS TO THE BACK OF YOUR
    HEAD.

CRISS-CROSS THE PANELS AT THE BACK OF YOUR
    NECK AND **BRING** THEM FORWARD TO
    THE FRONT UNDER YOUR CHIN.

TIE A SQUARE KNOT.

TUCK IN THE ENDS ON EACH SIDE.

PULL THE SCARF DOWN FROM
    YOUR NOSE AND **SPREAD**
    IT OVER THE KNOT.

A VARIATION TO THIS DESIGN IS
DONE WITH A VERY LARGE
SQUARE SCARF.   **FOLD** IT INTO A
TRIANGLE AND PLACE THE FOLD
UNDER YOUR CHIN. THEN
CONTINUE AS ABOVE.

FOLD A LARGE SQUARE SCARF INTO A
TRIANGLE.
PLACE THE FOLDED EDGE AROUND YOUR
NECK, MAKE SURE THE ENDS
ARE EVEN.
PINCH THE CENTRE OF THE FOLDED
EDGES TOGETHER.

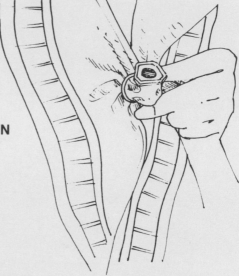

PUSH THE PINCHED EDGES **DOWN**
THROUGH THE LOOP OF
YOUR SCARF CLIP,
ABOUT THREE INCHES (7.5 cm).

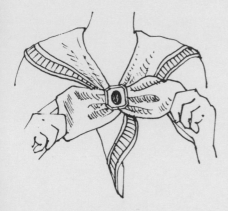

SEPARATE THE FOLDS, TAKING ONE
TO THE LEFT AND ONE TO THE
RIGHT.
FLUFF EACH BOW FROM THE BACK OF
THE SCARF WITH YOUR FINGERTIPS.
CLOSE THE CLIP.

SPREAD EACH TRIANGLE BELOW THE
BOW TO FINISH.

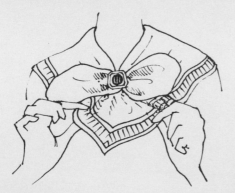

FOLD A SQUARE SCARF ON THE BIAS TO ABOUT 3 INCHES (7.5 cm) WIDE.

MAKE A LOOSE KNOT IN THE CENTRE. THEN MAKE TWO ADDITIONAL KNOTS ON EACH SIDE OF THE CENTRE KNOT TO MAKE A TOTAL OF 5 KNOTS.

PLACE THE SCARF AROUND THE NECK AS A NECKLACE.

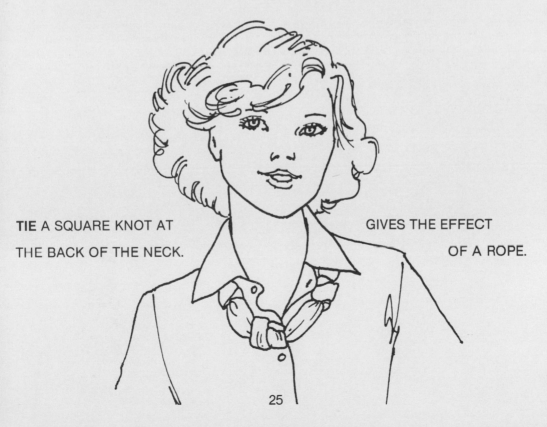

TIE A SQUARE KNOT AT THE BACK OF THE NECK.

GIVES THE EFFECT OF A ROPE.

FOLD A MEDIUM SQUARE SCARF IN HALF INTO A
RECTANGLE THEN FOLD IN HALF AGAIN,
LENGTHWISE, UNTIL THE SCARF IS ABOUT
FIVE INCHES (12.7 cm) WIDE.

PLACE THE SCARF AROUND YOUR NECK WITH
THE FOLDED EDGE NEXT TO YOUR NECK.

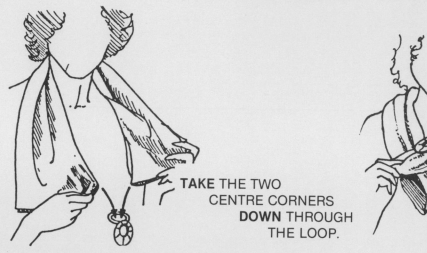

TAKE THE TWO
CENTRE CORNERS
DOWN THROUGH
THE LOOP.

KEEP PULLING THE BOTTOM EDGES THROUGH
UNTIL THE OUTER CORNERS HAVE
PASSED THROUGH THE LOOP OF THE CLIP.

MAKE SURE THE SCARF ENDS ARE EVEN,
SPREAD THE ENDS NICELY.
CLOSE THE CLIP.

THIS DESIGN MAKES YOUR SQUARE SCARF LOOK LIKE
AN OBLONG SCARF.

98

TAKE AN OBLONG SCARF AND **FOLD** IT LENGTHWISE IN THIRDS.

FOLD THE SCARF IN HALF AND **PLACE** IT AROUND YOUR NECK.

OPEN THE LOOP FORMED BY THE CENTER FOLD, **SEND** THE TWO ENDS **DOWN** THROUGH THE LOOP.

SLIDE THE LOOP UP BY PULLING THE ENDS DOWN.

THIS DESIGN CAN BE WORN ON THE SHOULDER, WITH ONE PANEL TO THE BACK AND THE OTHER TO THE FRONT.

A VARIATION: FOLLOW THE FIRST THREE STEPS BUT KEEP THE SCARF DRAPED LOOSELY AROUND THE NECK.

A VARIATION OF THE DESIGN ON THE PRECEDING PAGE.

FOR A SMALLER RUFFLE,

OPEN THE CLIP AND SLIDE IT DOWN
ABOUT FOUR TO SIX INCHES.
(10.2 - 15.3 cm)

CLOSE THE CLIP WHEN THE RUFFLE IS
THE SIZE YOU LIKE.

STILL ANOTHER DESIGN, CONTINUING FROM THE

PRECEDING PAGE ...

FOR A 'MUFFLED' LOOK, TAKE BOTH

ENDS AND **TWIST** THEM AROUND THE

SCARF ON THE SIDE.

OR

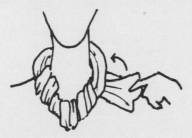

SEPARATE THE PANELS AND

TWIST EACH ONE

AROUND EACH SIDE

OF THE SCARF.

LOVELY WITH
TEXTURED SCARVES.

FOLD A MEDIUM SQUARE SCARF IN HALF INTO A RECTANGLE.

PLACE THE SCARF AROUND YOUR NECK WITH THE OUTSIDE EDGES, NOT THE FOLD, NEXT TO YOUR NECK.

TAKE THE CENTRE CORNERS (THE FOUR CORNERS OF THE SCARF) **DOWN** THROUGH THE LOOP OF THE CLIP.

SLIDE THE CLIP UP, ALMOST TO YOUR NECK.

PULL THE BOTTOM EDGES OF THE RECTANGLE THROUGH USING THUMBS AND INDEX FINGERS UNTIL HALF THE BOTTOM EDGE IS THROUGH THE CLIP.

CLOSE THE CLIP.

FOR A FULLER LOOK ...

OPEN THE CLIP AGAIN AND CONTINUE TO **PULL** THE BOTTOM EDGES ALL THE WAY THROUGH THE CLIP UNTIL THE OUTER CORNERS PASS THROUGH THE LOOP.

SPREAD FULLY TO FORM A 'FAN' LOOK.

CLOSE THE CLIP.

HOLD ONE END OF THE SCARF AND
TWIRL IT WITH YOUR WRIST.

PICK UP THE OTHER END QUICKLY
AND **HOLD** BOTH ENDS IN ONE
HAND. THE SCARF WILL WIND
ITSELF UP.

PLACE THE FOLDED TWISTED SCARF
AROUND THE NECK.

PUT THE TWO ENDS THROUGH
THE LOOP.

THIS DESIGN ACCENTS THE
BORDER OF YOUR SCARF.

FOLD A MEDIUM SQUARE SCARF INTO A TRIANGLE.

PLACE THE TRIANGLE AT THE FRONT.

TAKE THE TWO ENDS TO THE BACK.

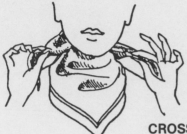

CROSS THE ENDS AT THE BACK AND BRING THEM FORWARD TO THE FRONT.

TAKE THE TWO ENDS **DOWN** THROUGH THE LOOP OF YOUR SCARF CLIP.

SLIDE THE CLIP UP, PULLING THE SCARF THROUGH.

SPREAD THE ENDS OUT TO THE

SIDES AND **CLOSE** THE CLIP.

TRY THIS ONE AS A FILLER AT THE NECK OF A BLOUSE OR BLAZER, TUCK IN THE TRIANGLE, LETTING THE TWO ENDS BE THE FEATURE.

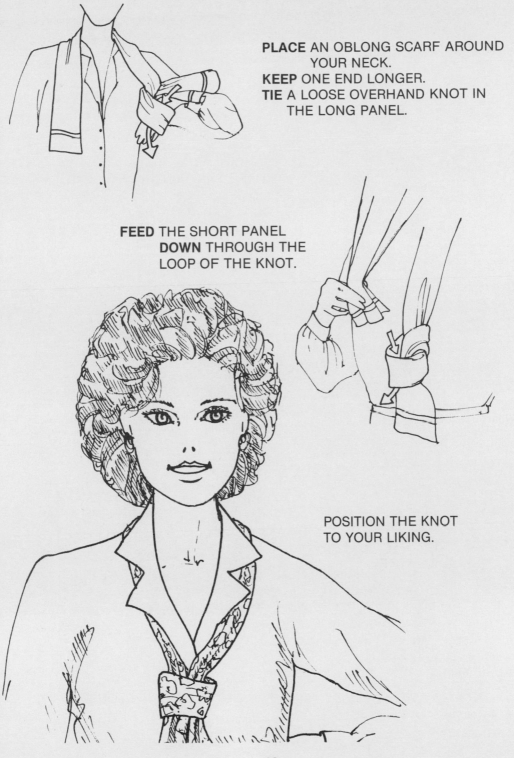

PLACE AN OBLONG SCARF AROUND YOUR NECK.
KEEP ONE END LONGER.
TIE A LOOSE OVERHAND KNOT IN THE LONG PANEL.

FEED THE SHORT PANEL
DOWN THROUGH THE
LOOP OF THE KNOT.

POSITION THE KNOT
TO YOUR LIKING.

PLACE A SAFETY PIN IN THE UNDERSIDE OF YOUR BLOUSE OR SWEATER CREATING A BAR FOR YOUR SCARF CLIP.
FOLD A MEDIUM SQUARE SCARF IN HALF INTO A TRIANGLE.
PLACE THE FOLDED EDGE AROUND YOUR NECK.

FEED ONE PANEL (A) **DOWN** THROUGH THE LOOP OF YOUR SCARF CLIP.
PLACE THE CLIP LOOP THROUGH THE SAFETY PIN BAR.
FEED THE OTHER PANEL (B) **DOWN** THROUGH THE CLIP LOOP.

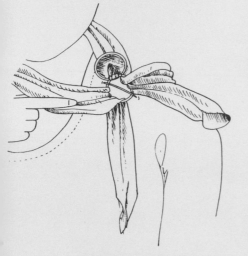

SPREAD THE PANELS AND **CLOSE** THE CLIP.

THIS DESIGN IS A FAVOURITE BECAUSE IT WILL ALWAYS STAY IN PLACE.

VARIATION: USE THE SAME SCARF, BUT ROLL IT UNTIL IT IS ABOUT FOUR INCHES (10.2 cm) WIDE.

94

PLACE AN OBLONG SCARF ON A FLAT SURFACE

FOLD IT IN HALF.

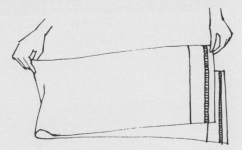

WITH YOUR FINGER TIPS ON THE OPPOSITE DIAGONAL CORNERS **LIFT** UP THE SCARF.   NOTE HOW THIS SHAPES TWO TRIANGLES.

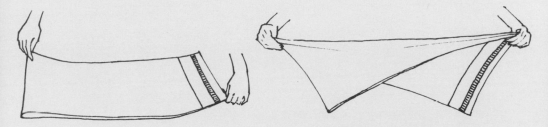

PLACE THE FOLDED EDGE AROUND YOUR NECK, KEEPING THE ENDS EVEN.

TIE A SQUARE KNOT.

LOVELY AS A SAILOR COLLAR WORN AS SHOWN.   FOR A COUPLE OF VARIATIONS, SEE THE NEXT PAGE.

AN INTERESTING VARIATION
OF THE DESIGN ON THE PRECEDING PAGE

TO CREATE A JABOT WITH A FULLER PUFF ...

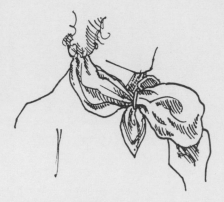

OPEN THE SCARF CLIP.

CONTINUE TO **PULL** THE SCARF THROUGH
THE CLIP UNTIL THERE IS JUST A SMALL
PART OF THE TRIANGLE LEFT.

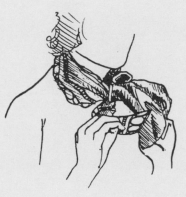

TUCK THE REMAINING TRIANGLE INTO
THE BACK OF THE PUFF. **FORM**
A POCKET WITH THE PUFF.

CLOSE THE CLIP.

NICE WITH A BLOUSE.

REALLY FINISHES OFF YOUR ATTIRE.

FOLD, PLACE, AND **TIE** YOUR OBLONG SCARF AS SHOWN ON THE PRECEDING PAGE, BUT ...

WEAR IT OFF TO THE SIDE.

THIS WAY YOU FEATURE THE

BORDER OF THE SCARF.

WEAR THE KNOT AT THE

BACK AND YOU CAPTURE

THE CENTRE OF THE

SCARF DESIGN.

FOR A DRESSIER LOOK,
ADD YOUR FAVOURITE SCARF CLIP.

FOLD A SQUARE SCARF INTO A TRIANGLE.

PLACE THE FOLDED EDGE AROUND YOUR
         NECK, MAKING SURE THE ENDS
         ARE EVEN.

TIE A SQUARE KNOT WITH THE ENDS.

PLACE THE KNOT TO THE BACK OF YOUR NECK.

TAKE A 'PINCH' OF THE FOLDED EDGE THAT'S
         NOW UNDER YOUR CHIN.

SEND IT **DOWN** THROUGH THE LOOP
         OF THE SCARF CLIP.

PULL THROUGH ENOUGH SCARF TO MAKE A PUFF.

SPREAD THE PUFF WITH YOUR
           FINGERS.

CLOSE THE SCARF CLIP.

TO BE WORN AS A SUIT FILLER.

THIS DESIGN WILL FEATURE
THE CENTRE OF YOUR SCARF.

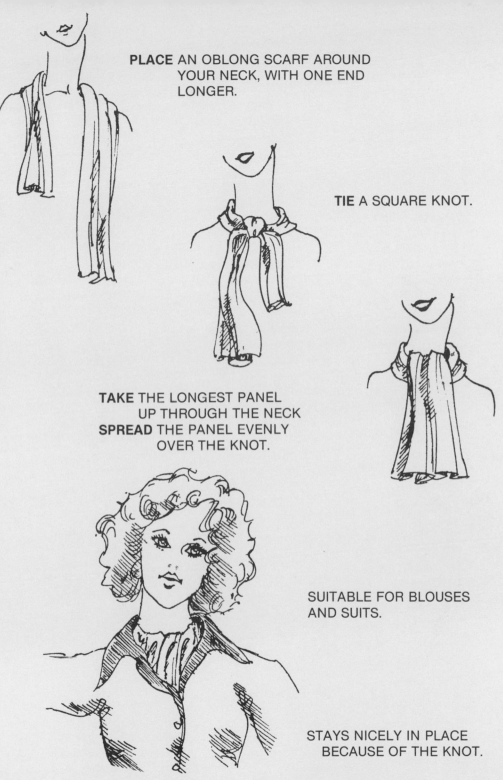

PLACE AN OBLONG SCARF AROUND
YOUR NECK, WITH ONE END
LONGER.

TIE A SQUARE KNOT.

TAKE THE LONGEST PANEL
UP THROUGH THE NECK
SPREAD THE PANEL EVENLY
OVER THE KNOT.

SUITABLE FOR BLOUSES
AND SUITS.

STAYS NICELY IN PLACE
BECAUSE OF THE KNOT.

A VARIATION OF THE PRECEDING DESIGN TO ACCENT THE BORDER OF YOUR SCARF.

PICK UP ALL THE OUTSIDE EDGES OF THE SCARF AND

BRING THEM TO THE CENTRE, **HOLD** THEM IN ONE HAND.

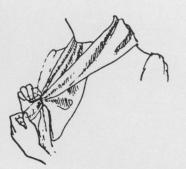

SEND THE PINCHED EDGES **DOWN** THROUGH THE LOOP OF YOUR SCARF CLIP.

SEPARATE ALL THE PINCHED EDGES.

PULL EACH PUFF SEPARATELY TO FORM FOUR PETALS.

91

PLACE AN OBLONG SCARF AROUND

YOUR NECK, KEEPING ONE PANEL LONGER.

TIE A SQUARE KNOT.

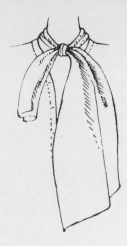

TAKE THE LONG PANEL UP THROUGH THE NECK AND

SPREAD IT EVENLY OVER THE KNOT.

WITH YOUR RIGHT HAND, **PICK** UP THE

MIDDLE OF THE

LONG PANEL AND

WRAP IT AROUND

THE FIRST BUTTON.

SEND THE BUTTON AND

SCARF THROUGH THE

BUTTON HOLE.

REPEAT FOR EVERY

BUTTON.

A UNIQUE WAY TO DRESS UP A CARDIGAN.

33

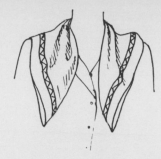

FOLD A SQUARE SCARF INTO A
TRIANGLE AND **PLACE** IT
AROUND YOUR SHOULDERS.

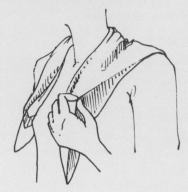

PICK UP THE TOP PANEL OF THE OUTSIDE
EDGES AND BRING THEM TOGETHER
AT THE CENTRE.
PINCH THE EDGES TOGETHER
IN ONE HAND.

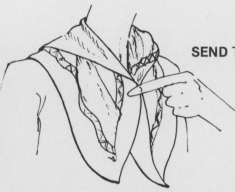

SEND THE PINCHED EDGES **DOWN** THROUGH

THE LOOP OF THE SCARF CLIP.

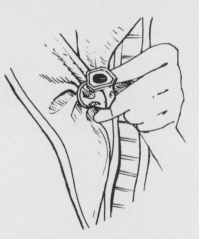

SEPARATE THE PINCHED EDGES AND
PULL EACH PUFF TO FORM A BOW.

THIS DESIGN EMPHASIZES
THE BORDER OF YOUR
SCARF. TRY THIS ONE
WITH AN OVERSIZE SCARF.

TAKE AN OBLONG SCARF AND **FOLD** IT IN THIRDS LENGTHWISE.

PLACE THE SCARF IN THE FRONT OF YOUR
NECK AND **TAKE** THE PANELS TO
THE BACK.
CRISS-CROSS THE PANELS AT THE BACK
AND **BRING** THEM FORWARD.

LEAVE ONE PANEL LONGER.

PLACE THE LONGER PANEL OVER THE
SHORT ONE.

TIE AN OVERHAND KNOT.

SMOOTH THE PANELS.

ADD A PEARL OR CHAIN NECKLACE
FOR ADDED INTEREST.

34

TO WEAR UNDER A COAT, COMPLETE THE DESIGN
ON THE PREVIOUS PAGE AND ...

OPEN THE CLIP AND **SLIDE** IT
ALL THE WAY UP THE SCARF TO
YOUR NECK.

SPREAD THE PANELS AS SHOWN.

CLOSE THE CLIP.

YOU CAN ALSO USE THIS DESIGN AS A HEAD COVERING.

TAKE AN OBLONG WOOLEN TEXTURED SCARF.

PLACE IT AROUND YOUR NECK AND

TIE AN OVERHAND KNOT.

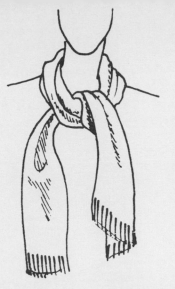

TAKE EACH PANEL AND **WIND** THEM

AROUND THE NECK AREA OF THE SCARF.

GIVES A ROPE EFFECT.

ADD A NICE TOUCH WHEN WORN
ON THE OUTSIDE OF A CASUAL
JACKET.

FOLD A SQUARE SCARF IN HALF INTO A RECTANGLE.

LAY THE SCARF ON A FLAT SURFACE, **PICK** UP
TWO OPPOSITE CORNERS AND FORM TWO TRIANGLES.

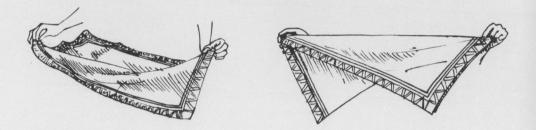

PLACE THE SCARF AROUND YOUR NECK, KEEP ENDS EVEN.

TAKE THE TWO ENDS **DOWN** THROUGH THE LOOP OF THE CLIP.

SLIDE THE CLIP UP THE ENDS ABOUT FOUR
OR FIVE INCHES (10 - 12.7 cm) AND **CLOSE** THE CLIP.

SPREAD EACH PANEL NICELY, PARTICULARLY
NEAR THE CLIP.

GREAT ON A SWEATER OR DRESS WITH NO COLLAR.

USE AN OBLONG OR BIAS SCARF.

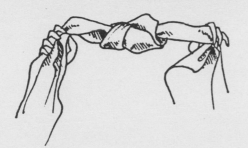

TIE A SINGLE KNOT AT THE
AT THE CENTRE OF
THE SCARF.

PLACE THE KNOT AT THE FRONT
OF YOUR NECK.
TAKE THE PANELS TO THE BACK.
CRISS-CROSS THE PANELS AND
BRING THEM FORWARD.
PULL THE ENDS THROUGH
THE KNOT AND **TIGHTEN.**

NICELY WORN IN THE FRONT
OR CAN BE WORN TO THE
SIDE.

FOLD A SQUARE SCARF INTO A TRIANGLE.

PLACE THE FOLDED EDGE AROUND YOUR NECK, MAKE SURE THE TWO ENDS ARE EVEN.

TAKE THE ENDS **DOWN** THROUGH THE LOOP OF YOUR SCARF CLIP. **SLIDE** THE CLIP UP TO YOUR NECK. DO NOT CLOSE THE CLIP YET.

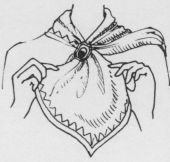

TAKE ONE PANEL TO THE SIDE.

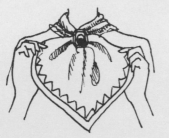

SPREAD THE OTHER PANEL IN FRONT AND THEN TAKE THE SIDE PANEL AND **SPREAD** IT EVENLY ON TOP OF THE FIRST PANEL. **CLOSE** THE CLIP.

CAN BE WORN NICELY LIKE THIS WITH BLOUSES AND COATS. BUT, FOR A FULLER ASCOT, YOU CAN ...

TAKE THE BOTTOM PANEL AND FEED IT UP THROUGH THE NECK AND BACK DOWN OVER THE TOP OF THE CLIP.

YOU WILL NOT SEE THE CLIP BUT YOU WILL ACHIEVE A FULLER WIDER ASCOT.

TAKE AN OBLONG SCARF AND **PLACE** IT AROUND YOUR NECK.

KEEPING ONE PANEL LONGER, **TIE** AN OVERHAND KNOT.

WITH YOUR FINGERTIPS
UNDER THE PANEL, THUMBS
ON **TOP, PLEAT** THE LONGER
PANEL UP TO THE KNOT.

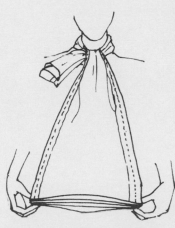

WRAP THE SHORT END AROUND
THE PLEATED ONE.

INSERT THE SHORT END THROUGH
THE LOOP YOU'VE FORMED
AND **PULL** TO TIGHTEN.

THIS DESIGN IS LOVELY AS SHOWN,

OR FOR A SLIGHTLY DIFFERENT

APPEARANCE, SEE THE NEXT PAGE.

FOR AN INTERESTING VARIATION USING A SCARF
CLIP WITH AN OPEN FACE, COMPLETE THE DESIGN
SHOWN ON THE PRECEDING PAGE, THEN ...

OPEN THE CLIP.

TAKE THE LONGER (BOTTOM) PANEL BACK
UP THROUGH THE NECK.

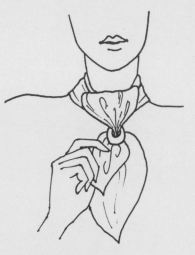

TAKE IT DOWN THROUGH THE OPEN FACE
OF YOUR SCARF CLIP.

SPREAD THIS PANEL AND **CLOSE** THE CLIP.

AN EXCELLENT WAY TO SECURE A SMALL SCARF.

A VARIATION OF THE DESIGN SHOWN ON THE PRECEDING PAGE.

USE A BIAS SCARF INSTEAD OF AN OBLONG ONE AND

TIE THE KNOT AT A LOWER POSITION.

FOLD A SMALL SQUARE SCARF INTO A TRIANGLE.

PLACE THE FOLDED EDGE AROUND YOUR NECK.
KEEP ONE END SLIGHTLY LONGER.

TAKE BOTH ENDS OF THE SCARF **DOWN**
THROUGH THE LOOP OF THE CLIP.

SLIDE THE CLIP UP THE SCARF TO
YOUR NECK, BUT DON'T
CLOSE THE CLIP YET.

SPREAD THE LONGEST PANEL.

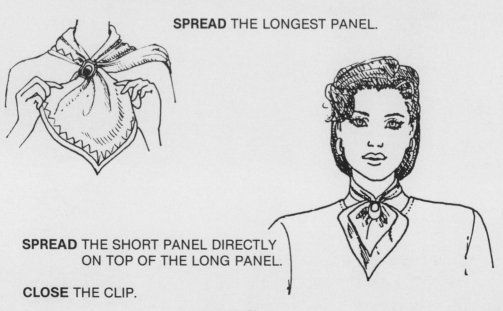

SPREAD THE SHORT PANEL DIRECTLY
ON TOP OF THE LONG PANEL.

CLOSE THE CLIP.

PLACE A BIAS SCARF LOOSELY IN THE FRONT OF YOUR NECK AND **TAKE** THE PANELS TO THE BACK.

CRISS-CROSS THE PANELS AND **BRING** THEM FORWARD.

TIE A SQUARE KNOT AT THE ENDS.
MAKE THE TWO LOOPS EQUAL IN SIZE.
SPREAD THE PANELS.

WEAR OFF TO THE SIDE.

VARIATION: FOLLOW THE FIRST STEP ABOVE AND FORM A 'PUFF' WITH THE CENTRE OF THE SCARF.

TAKE THE ENDS UNDER THE PUFF AND **CRISS-CROSS.**

BRING THE ENDS BACK OVER THE PUFF AND **TIE** A SQUARE KNOT.

SOME VARIATIONS ON THE PRECEDING DESIGN.

FOR A FLOWER, USE A POLYESTER SQUARE. AFTER COMPLETING ALL THE STEPS SHOWN ON THE PREVIOUS PAGE, **BEND** THE STITCHED EDGES BACKWARDS.

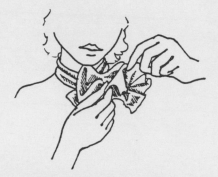

FOR ANOTHER VARIATION, TAKE TWO DIFFERENT COLOURED CHIFFON SCARVES AND PLEAT THEM TOGETHER AS SHOWN ON THE PREVIOUS PAGE.

SINCE THERE IS A LOT OF FABRIC IN THIS DESIGN, YOU MUST HOLD THE PLEATED ENDS TIGHTLY SO THE SCARVES WILL FIT DOWN THE LOOP OF THE CLIP.

FOR A BIAS OR OBLONG SCARF.

PLACE THE SCARF AROUND YOUR NECK

LEAVING ONE PANEL LONGER.

TIE A SQUARE KNOT.

FEED SOME OF THE LONGER

PANEL UP BEHIND THE

SQUARE KNOT. THIS

FORMS A "PUFF".

LET THE PUFF SIT OVER THE

TOP OF THE KNOT. **SPREAD** AND

ARRANGE THE PUFF.

VARIATION: FOLLOW THE INSTRUCTIONS

ABOVE, EXCEPT ... HAVE THE ENDS

EVEN BEFORE TYING THE SQUARE KNOT,

AND BRING BOTH PANELS UP THROUGH

THE NECK TO FORM TWO PUFFS.

PLEAT ONE EDGE OF A SMALL CHIFFON OR SILK SCARF.

HOLD THE PLEATS TOGETHER IN ONE HAND.

RUN YOUR OTHER HAND DOWN THE SCARF TO THE OTHER END.

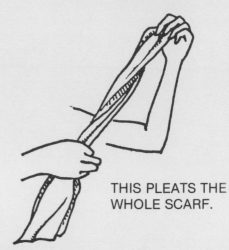

THIS PLEATS THE WHOLE SCARF.

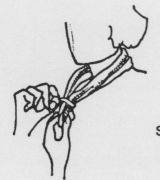

PLACE THE PLEATED SCARF AROUND YOUR NECK.

SEND BOTH ENDS OF THE PLEATED SCARF **DOWN** THROUGH THE LOOP OF THE SCARF CLIP.

SPREAD AND **FLUFF** OUT THE SCARF ENDS. **CLOSE** THE CLIP.

YOU CAN WEAR THIS AT THE FRONT OR TO THE SIDE.

VERY FEMININE AND DRESSY FOR EVENING WEAR.

FOLD A BIAS SCARF IN HALF AND **PLACE** IT AROUND YOUR NECK

FEED BOTH ENDS **DOWN** THROUGH THE LOOP YOU HAVE FORMED.

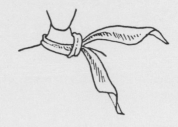

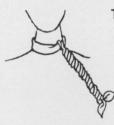

TIE THE TIPS OF
THE SCARF
TOGETHER.

TWIST THE PANELS.

WRAP THE TWISTED
SCARF AROUND THE
LOOPED AREA.

TUCK THE RABBIT EAR
KNOT INTO THE CENTRE
OF THE DESIGN FROM
THE BACK.

A NICE VARIATION, **TAKE** JUST ONE
PANEL THROUGH THE LOOP.

TIE A SQUARE KNOT WITH THE ENDS.

ARRANGE THE DESIGN OFF TO THE SIDE
TO FORM AN ATTRACTIVE RING.

VERY NICE FOR A WOMAN WITH A SHORT NECK.

FOR A DIFFERENT LOOK TO YOUR TWO SCARVES,
KNOT THEM TOGETHER AS SHOWN ON THE PREVIOUS
PAGE, AND **PLACE** THEM AROUND YOUR NECK WITH
THE KNOT AT THE BACK.

WRAP THE SCARVES AROUND YOUR NECK AS MANY
TIMES AS POSSIBLE, LEAVING ENDS ABOUT
SIX TO SEVEN INCHES (15.3 - 17.7 cm) LONG.

PLACE THE ENDS OF THE SCARVES **DOWN**
THROUGH THE LOOP OF THE CLIP.

SLIDE THE CLIP UP TO YOUR NECK.

CLOSE THE CLIP.

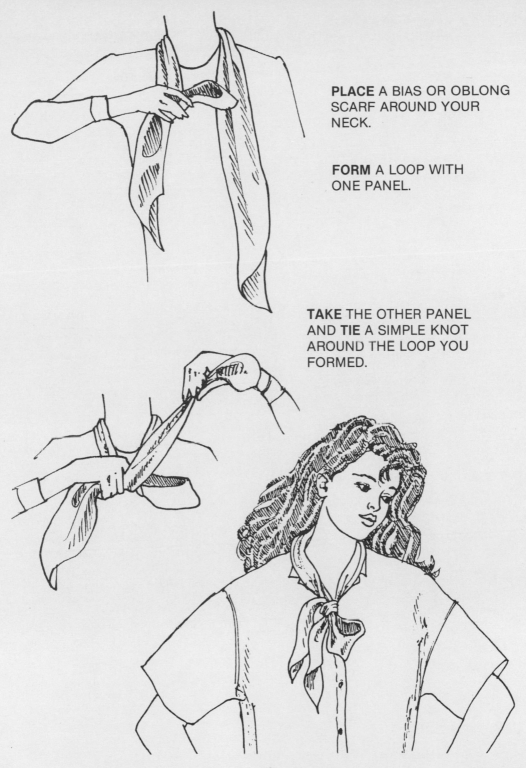

PLACE A BIAS OR OBLONG SCARF AROUND YOUR NECK.

FORM A LOOP WITH ONE PANEL.

TAKE THE OTHER PANEL AND **TIE** A SIMPLE KNOT AROUND THE LOOP YOU FORMED.

TAKE TWO SMALL SQUARE SCARVES OF
DIFFERENT COLOURS AND **KNOT**
TOGETHER AT ONE CORNER.

PLACE AROUND YOUR SHOULDERS WITH
THE KNOT AT THE BACK. **SHAPE**
SCARVES INTO TWO TRIANGLES
WITH THE FOLDED EDGES TO
THE CENTRE.

PINCH THE CENTRE OF
THE FOLDED EDGES
TOGETHER AND TAKE
THEM **DOWN** THROUGH THE
LOOP OF THE SCARF CLIP.

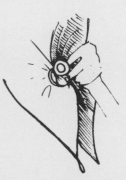

PLACE YOUR THUMB AND INDEX FINGER AT
THE BACK OF EACH 'PINCH', PULLING
THEM THROUGH AND SHAPING THE BOW.

CLOSE THE CLIP.

TAKE A LONG BIAS OR OBLONG SCARF,
TIE A LOOSE SINGLE KNOT ABOUT 4
TO 6 INCHES (10-15.5 cm) FROM ONE END.

WORKING WITH THE LONGER PANEL,
FORM A LOOP NEAR THE KNOT AND
FEED IT UP THROUGH THE KNOT.

CONTINUE MAKING LOOPS TO FORM
A CHAIN LEAVING ABOUT 6 TO 8
INCHES (15-20.5 cm) FOR FINISHING.

TAKE THIS END AND SEND IT UP THROUGH THE
LAST LOOP TO SECURE THE DESIGN.

DEPENDING ON THE LENGTH OF YOUR SCARF, AND THE
NUMBER OF LOOPS YOU'VE MADE, THIS
DESIGN MAY BE WORN AROUND
YOUR NECK,
HEAD, OR
WAIST.

43

FOR A PRETTY VARIATION ON THE
PRECEDING DESIGN, MAKE A FULL
BUTTERFLY.

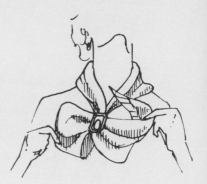

COMPLETE THE STEPS AS SHOWN, BUT,

TAKE THE SECOND TIP **DOWN** THE LOOP FOR AN INCH OR TWO.
(2.5 - 5 cm)

SPREAD BOTH SIDES OF THE BOW.

CLOSE THE CLIP.

USE A BIAS SCARF
LAID OUT ON A FLAT SURFACE.

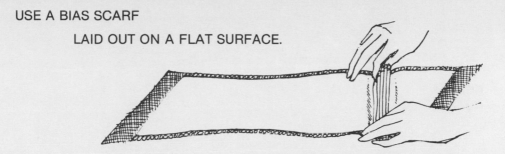

STARTING ABOUT 10
INCHES (25 cm) FROM ONE END,
PLEAT THE SCARF WITH
YOUR FINGERTIPS TO
ABOUT THE SAME
POSITION FROM THE
OTHER END.

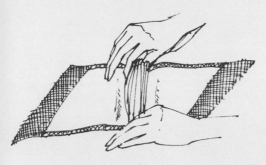

HOLD THE PLEATS SECURELY, **TAKE**
THE TWO ENDS AND **TWIST** THEM TWICE.

TURN THE SCARF OVER AND
TIE A SQUARE KNOT TO
SECURE YOUR DESIGN.

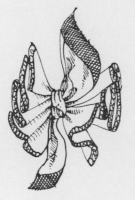

TIE THE ENDS AT THE BACK
OF YOUR NECK.
FLUFF AND ARRANGE THE SCARF.

FOLD A SMALL SQUARE SCARF INTO A TRIANGLE.

PLACE THE FOLDED EDGE AROUND YOUR NECK.
KEEP THE ENDS EVEN.

BRING BOTH ENDS OF THE
SCARF **DOWN** THROUGH
THE LOOP OF THE CLIP.

SLIDE THE CLIP UP THE SCARF TO YOUR
NECK, BUT DON'T CLOSE IT YET.

CROSS THE PANELS BELOW THE CLIP SO THE
FOLDED EDGES ARE ON THE OUTSIDE.

TAKE ONE TIP OF THE SCARF AND FEED
IT **DOWN** THE LOOP AGAIN, JUST AN
INCH OR TWO (2.5 - 5 cm).

SPREAD THE HALF BOW.

CLOSE THE CLIP.

YOU CAN TAKE THIS DESIGN TO
THE SIDE OR SHOULDER.

A VARIATION:

FOLLOW THE INSTRUCTIONS ON THE PRECEDING PAGE AND **PLEAT** THE SCARF.

HOLDING THE PLEATS IN ONE HAND, **STRETCH** AN ELASTIC BAND OVER THE PLEATS, WORK IT TO THE CENTRE.

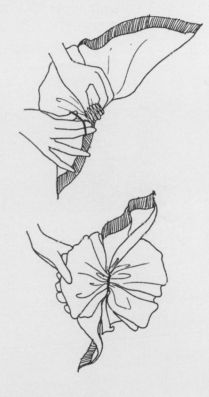

FOLD THE PLEATS SO THE ELASTIC BAND ISN'T VISIBLE. THIS FORMS A DOUBLE RUFFLE.

ROLL A SMALL OR MEDIUM SQUARE SCARF
UNTIL IT IS ABOUT THREE INCHES (7.5 cm) WIDE.

PLACE THE SCARF AROUND YOUR NECK.

TAKE BOTH ENDS **DOWN** THROUGH
THE LOOP OF THE CLIP.

SLIDE THE CLIP UP TO YOUR NECK,
PULLING THE ENDS THROUGH.
CLOSE THE CLIP.

TAKE THE ENDS BACK AROUND YOUR NECK,
ONE END TO EACH SIDE.

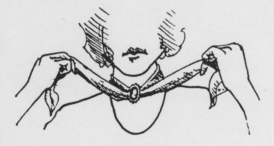

TUCK THE ENDS
IN NEATLY.

FORMS A CHOKER.

FOR EVENING WEAR.

78

ANOTHER VARIATION:

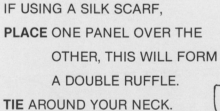

INSTEAD OF USING AN ELASTIC
BAND, USE A SCARF CLIP AND
SEND ONE END OF THE PLEATS
DOWN THROUGH THE LOOP
OF THE CLIP.
PUSH THE CLIP TO THE CENTRE
OF THE SCARF AND
CLOSE THE CLIP.

IF USING A SILK SCARF,
PLACE ONE PANEL OVER THE
OTHER, THIS WILL FORM
A DOUBLE RUFFLE.
TIE AROUND YOUR NECK.

FOLD A SQUARE SCARF ON THE BIAS (POINTS TO THE CENTRE) UNTIL ABOUT FOUR INCHES (10.2 cm) WIDE.

PLACE THE FOLDED SCARF AROUND YOUR NECK, KEEPING THE ENDS EVEN.

TAKE BOTH ENDS OF THE SCARF **DOWN** THROUGH THE LOOP OF THE CLIP.

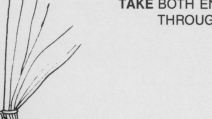

SPREAD EACH PANEL A LITTLE, TURN THE DESIGN TOWARDS THE SIDE (AS FAR AS YOU LIKE).

CLOSE THE CLIP.

TAKE ANY TYPE OF SCARF AND
PLACE IT AROUND YOUR NECK.

MAKE ONE PANEL (B) OF
THE SCARF LONGER.

TAKE (B) PANEL AND
CROSS IT OVER (A)
PANEL AND FEED IT UP
THROUGH THE NECK.

USING THE SAME PANEL (B),
CROSS OVER PANEL (A)
BELOW THE FIRST PART OF
THE KNOT,

AND BRING (B) UP
THROUGH THE
LITTLE OPENING.

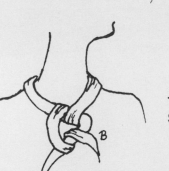

TIGHTEN THE KNOT AND
SPREAD THE PANELS.

THE SQUARE KNOT

47

TAKE A LONG NARROW SCARF AND **TIE** A LOOSE KNOT IN THE CENTRE.

PLACE THE KNOT ON THE TOP OF YOUR HEAD.

TAKE ONE PANEL BEHIND YOUR HEAD.

SEND BOTH ENDS OF THE SCARF **DOWN** THROUGH THE LOOP OF THE SCARF CLIP.

SLIDE THE CLIP UP TO YOUR EAR.

CLOSE THE CLIP.

VERY ATTRACTIVE TO WEAR FOR PATIO, PARTIES, BEACH WEAR, AND INFORMAL GATHERINGS.

PLACE AN OBLONG SCARF OR
A TIE AROUND YOUR NECK.

KEEP ONE END (B) SLIGHTLY
LONGER THAN THE OTHER (A).

BRING (B) PANEL OVER (A),
THEN UNDER, THEN OVER AGAIN.

BRING THE SAME PANEL (B) UP THROUGH
THE NECK AREA.

FEED IT DOWN THE FRONT THROUGH
THE OPENING OF THE
LOOP YOU'VE FORMED.

TO TIGHTEN THE KNOT
PULL PANEL (B).

THIS IS A VERY TAILORED
DESIGN FOR BLOUSES WORN
WITH SUITS AND VESTS.

FOLD A LARGE OBLONG SCARF IN HALF LENGTHWISE.

PLACE THE FOLDED EDGE AROUND YOUR NECK.

PASS BOTH ENDS OF THE SCARF **DOWN** THROUGH THE LOOP OF YOUR SCARF CLIP.

CLOSE THE CLIP ABOUT FOUR TO SIX INCHES (10.2 - 15.5 cm) FROM THE ENDS OF THE SCARF.

TAKE THE SCARF ABOVE THE CLIP AND, WITH YOUR FINGERS **REACH** UNDER THE FOLDS AND **SPREAD** THE SCARF INTO A SINGLE LAYER.

PLACE THE SCARF ON YOUR HEAD AND FOLD THE LEADING EDGE UNDER, ABOUT TWO INCHES (5 cm).

OPEN THE CLIP AND SLIDE IT TO THE NECK, THEN **CLOSE** AGAIN.

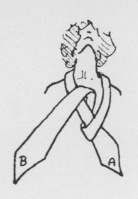

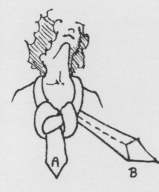

THE **WINDSOR KNOT**

A DESCRIPTION BEYOND WORDS

PLACE AN OBLONG SCARF AROUND YOUR HEAD.

TAKE ONE PANEL BEHIND YOUR HEAD.

PINCH THE EDGES OF THE SCARF
AND **FEED** THEM **DOWN**
THROUGH THE LOOP OF
YOUR SCARF CLIP.

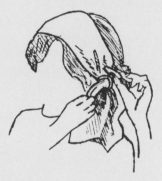

SEPARATE THE FOLDS YOU'VE BROUGHT THROUGH
THE CLIP TO FORM A NICE BOW.

SPREAD AND **FLUFF** WITH YOUR
FINGERTIPS.
CLOSE THE CLIP.

STILL LOOKING FOR THE WORDS TO DESCRIBE

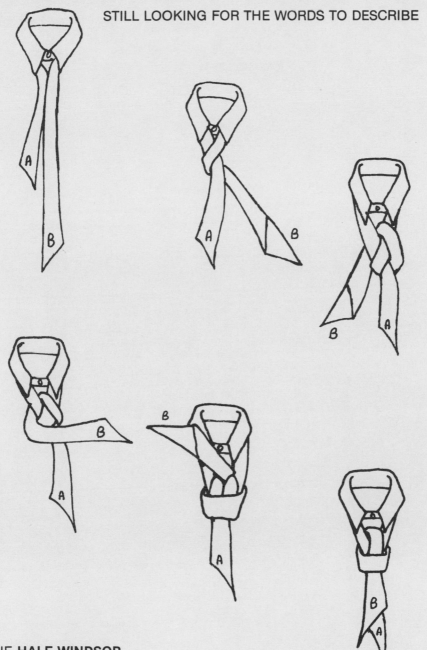

THE HALF WINDSOR

PLACE AN OBLONG SCARF AROUND YOUR HEAD.

TAKE ONE PANEL BEHIND YOUR HEAD.

PUT BOTH ENDS TOGETHER IN ONE HAND.

BRING THE ENDS OF THE SCARF **DOWN** THROUGH THE LOOP OF YOUR SCARF CLIP.

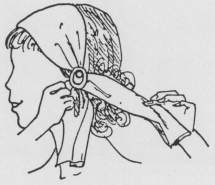

PULL THE TOP PANEL OF THE SCARF UNTIL THE SCARF CLIP IS AT THE EAR LEVEL.

CLOSE THE CLIP.

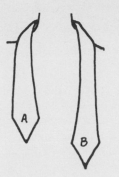

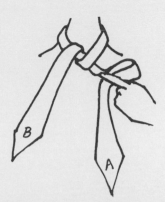

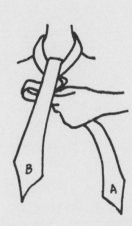

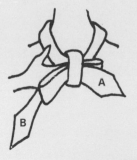

THE TRADITIONAL
BOW TIE

51

TAKE THE STRAIGHT EDGE OF A LARGE SQUARE SCARF, PREFERABLY CHIFFON, AND **PLEAT** IT AS SHOWN.

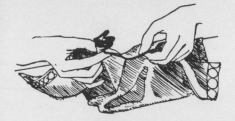

HOLD THE PLEATED END IN ONE HAND,

SLIDE YOUR OTHER HAND DOWN THE SCARF TO GATHER THE OTHER END.

PLACE THE GATHERED SCARF AROUND YOUR HEAD TAKING BOTH ENDS TO ONE SIDE.

TAKE BOTH PLEATED ENDS IN ONE HAND. **SEND** THEM **DOWN** THROUGH THE LOOP OF THE CLIP.

CLOSE THE CLIP AND **SPREAD** THE ENDS AROUND THE CLIP TO FORM A RUFFLE LOOK.

72

YOU CAN ACHIEVE DIFFERENT RESULTS WITH THE SAME SIMPLE STEPS, AS SHOWN ON THE PRECEDING PAGE, BY USING VARIOUS SIZE TIES OR SCARVES.

BEYOND THE BASIC BOW

FOLD A LARGE SQUARE SCARF IN
HALF INTO A RECTANGLE.

PLACE THE OUTSIDE EDGES,
NOT THE FOLD, NEXT
TO YOUR NECK.

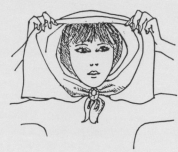

TAKE ALL FOUR CORNERS OF THE
SCARF IN YOUR HAND AND PUT THEM
DOWN THROUGH THE LOOP OF THE CLIP.

SLIDE THE CLIP UP THE SCARF FOUR OR FIVE INCHES
(10.2 - 12.7 cm) AND **CLOSE** THE CLIP.

TAKE THE FOLDED PANEL FROM THE
BACK AND BRING IT UP AND
FORWARD TO THE TOP OF YOUR HEAD.

FOLD THE LEADING EDGE BACK ABOUT
THREE INCHES (7.5 cm).

TAKE THE SIDES OF THE SCARF AND
TUCK INSIDE THE BONNET.

PULL THE ENDS OF THE SCARF UNTIL THE
BONNET FITS SNUGLY.

FLUFF OUT THE ENDS OF THE SCARF.

WITH AN ORDINARY BUCKLE YOU CAN CREATE
YOUR OWN INDIVIDUAL STYLES AT YOUR WAIST
OR NECK WITH COLOURFUL SCARVES.

SIMPLY **FEED** THE ENDS OF THE
SCARF THROUGH THE OPENINGS OF
THE BUCKLE ONE AT A TIME.

WEAR IN THE FRONT WITH THE ENDS OF THE
SCARF TUCKED IN OR YOU CAN ALSO WEAR AT
THE SIDE WITH THE SCARF ENDS HANGING SOFTLY.

FOLLOW THE SAME BASIC INSTRUCTIONS WITH
THE SCARF AT YOUR NECK.

FOLD A LARGE SQUARE SCARF IN HALF INTO A RECTANGLE. KEEP THE FOLDED EDGE NEXT TO YOU.

TAKE THE TOP PANEL OF THE FOLDED SCARF AND BRING **IT BACK TO THE** FOLDED EDGE. (HANG ON TO THOSE CORNERS!).

PICK UP BOTH THOSE CORNERS AND THE FOLDED EDGE.

TURN THE SCARF UPSIDE DOWN AND LAY IT FLAT.

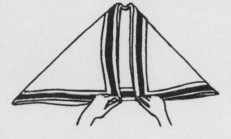

STILL HANGING ON TO THOSE TWO CORNERS, **BRING** THEM DOWN TO THE CENTRE TO FORM A TRIANGLE.

ROLL THE LONG BOTTOM EDGE SEVERAL TIMES TO HOLD THE DESIGN TOGETHER.

WITH YOUR HANDS CLOSE TO THE CENTRE OF THE ROLLED EDGE, **LIFT** YOUR BONNET.

PLACE THE BONNET ON YOUR HEAD WITH THE ROLLED EDGE AROUND YOUR NECK. **TIE** THE ENDS OR PUT THEM **DOWN** THROUGH YOUR SCARF CLIP.

70

FOLD A LARGE SQUARE SCARF ON THE BIAS TO ABOUT TEN INCHES WIDE. **TWIST** LOOSELY AND **WRAP** AROUND YOUR WAIST. **TIE** A KNOT AND **TUCK** IN THE ENDS.

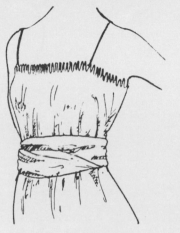

WRAP AN OBLONG SCARF AROUND YOUR WAIST. **TIE** A SQUARE KNOT. **TWIST** THE TWO ENDS TOGETHER AND **WRAP** THE TWISTED SCARF AROUND THE KNOT TO FORM A ROSE. **TUCK** THE ENDS INTO THE CENTRE OF THE FLOWER. IF NECESSARY, HOLD WITH A STRAIGHT PIN.

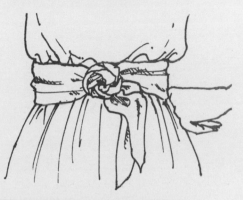

TIE A LOOSE KNOT IN THE MIDDLE OF AN OBLONG SCARF (OR A SQUARE FOLDED INTO A BIAS), **PLACE** AROUND YOUR WAIST, **TIE** A KNOT AT THE BACK AND **TUCK** IN THE ENDS.

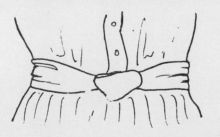

TAKE THREE OBLONG SCARVES AND **TIE** THEM TOGETHER AT ONE END. **BRAID,** THEN **TIE** THE OTHER END. **WRAP** AND **TIE** AROUND YOUR WAIST.

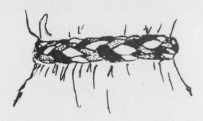

TO COMPLETE A 'PIRATE'S CAP', FOLLOW THE STEPS ON THE
PRECEDING PAGE, AND

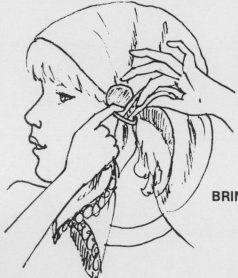

OPEN THE CLIP.

BRING THE BACK PANEL FORWARD
AND PUT IT **DOWN** THROUGH
THE LOOP OF THE SCARF CLIP

CLOSE THE CLIP AGAIN.

SPREAD EACH PANEL SEPARATELY
AND SMOOTHLY.

A GREAT HEAD COVERING!

GREAT WITH JEANS AND CASUAL WEAR.

TAKE TWO SQUARE SCARVES, LAY THEM ON A TABLE, SIDE BY SIDE, AS SHOWN IN THE FIRST DRAWING.
TIE A KNOT WITH THE TWO CORNERS.
FOLD THE TWO OUTSIDE CORNERS IN TOWARDS THE CENTRE KNOT.
PICK UP THE FOLDED SCARVES AND PLACE THE KNOT BETWEEN YOUR BREASTS.
TIE THE TOP CORNERS BEHIND YOUR NECK AND THE TWO BOTTOM CORNERS AT YOUR WAIST.

PICK UP A STRAIGHT EDGE OF A LARGE SQUARE SCARF AND **TIE** A KNOT BEHIND YOUR NECK. **TAKE** THE OTHER TWO ENDS AND **TIE** A KNOT BEHIND YOUR WAIST. **USE** A BELT OR ANOTHER SCARF AT THE WAIST TO FINISH.

TRY WEARING THIS DESIGN AS A BLOUSE UNDER A SUIT.

FOLD A MEDIUM SQUARE SCARF
INTO A TRIANGLE.

PLACE IT ON YOUR HEAD WITH THE
FOLDED EDGE AT THE FRONT.

TAKE ONE OF THE PANELS BEHIND YOUR HEAD.

WITH BOTH ENDS IN ONE HAND ...

PUT THE ENDS **DOWN** THROUGH THE LOOP
OF YOUR SCARF CLIP.

SLIDE THE CLIP UP THE
SCARF ENDS UNTIL
THE SCARF IS SNUG
ON YOUR HEAD.

CLOSE THE CLIP.

TAKE TWO OBLONG SCARVES
AND **TIE** ONE AROUND YOUR
BUST. **TAKE** THE SECOND
SCARF THROUGH THE FIRST
ONE AND **TIE** A KNOT
BEHIND YOUR NECK.

TAKE TWO BIAS TIES AND **TIE**
A SQUARE KNOT AT ONE END.
PLACE THE KNOT BETWEEN YOUR
BREASTS, **WRAP** THE SCARVES
AROUND YOUR BODICE, **CRISS
CROSS** AT THE BACK AND BRING
THE ENDS UNDER YOUR ARMS
TO THE FRONT. **TAKE** THE
ENDS BEHIND YOUR NECK AND
TIE A KNOT.

FOLD A MEDIUM OR LARGE SQUARE SCARF INTO A TRIANGLE.

PLACE THE FOLDED EDGE ON YOUR FOREHEAD JUST ABOVE YOUR EYES.

BRING THE SIDE PANELS TO THE BACK OF YOUR HEAD AND **TAKE** THE FOLDED EDGES IN ONE HAND.

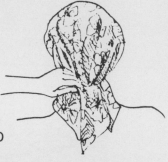

PINCH THE FOLDED EDGES TOGETHER AND **PUSH** THE PINCH **DOWN** THROUGH THE LOOP OF THE CLIP.

SEPARATE AND **SPREAD** EACH FOLD TO FORM A BOW.

CLOSE THE CLIP.

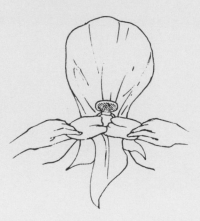

FOLD YOUR LARGE SQUARE SHAWL
IN HALF INTO A TRIANGLE.
DRAPE THE FOLDED SHAWL OVER
YOUR SHOULDER AND SECURE ONE
OR BOTH ENDS WITH A BELT

FOLD YOUR LARGE SQUARE SHAWL IN
HALF INTO A RECTANGLE. KEEP
FOLDING IT IN HALF UNTIL IT
IS ABOUT EIGHT INCHES (20.5 cm) WIDE.

DRAPE THE FOLDED SHAWL OVER ONE
SHOULDER AND SECURE ONE OR
BOTH ENDS AT YOUR WAIST
WITH A BELT.

BOTH OF THESE SHAWL DESIGNS
CAN BE WORN WITH ANY ENSEMBLE.

FOLD AND LINK YOUR TWO SCARVES

AS SHOWN ON THE PRECEDING PAGE.

AFTER PLACING THE LINK ON THE TOP OF YOUR HEAD.

TAKE BOTH PANELS BEHIND YOUR HEAD AND
FEED ALL THE ENDS **DOWN** THROUGH
THE LOOP OF THE CLIP.

CLOSE THE CLIP.

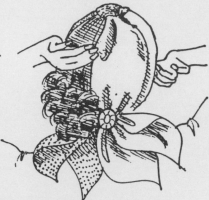

SEPARATE AND **SPREAD** THE FOLDED
PANELS TOWARD THE CENTRE.

A VERY DRESSY TURBAN, CAN BE WORN
AT GARDEN PARTIES.

VERY FUNCTIONAL FOR CRUISES AND
HOLIDAYS.

FOLD A LARGE SQUARE SHAWL IN HALF INTO A
RECTANGLE WITH RIGHT SIDES TOGETHER.

TIE TWO RABBIT EAR KNOTS AT THE CORNERS AS SHOWN.

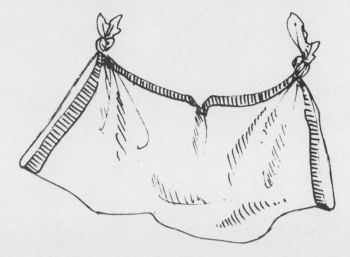

TURN THE SHAWL RIGHT SIDE OUT AND **PLACE** YOUR ARMS
THROUGH THE OPENINGS CREATED BY THE KNOTTED
CORNERS. THE KNOTS SHOULD BE UNDER YOUR ARMS
SO THEY CAN'T BE SEEN.

YOUR SHAWL WON'T SLIP
OFF YOUR SHOULDER.

TRY THIS WITH
YOUR FAVOURITE
SUIT OR COAT.

58

TAKE TWO SQUARE SCARVES AND

    FOLD EACH TO ABOUT FOUR INCHES (10.2 cm) WIDE.

    PLACE ONE ON TOP OF THE
OTHER TO FORM A CROSS.

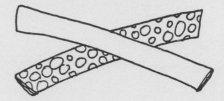

    PICK UP THE BOTTOM SCARF BY THE
ENDS, THIS WILL FORM A LINK.

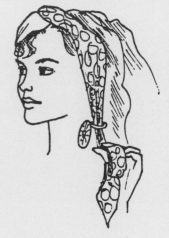

    PLACE THE LINK ON THE
    TOP OF YOUR HEAD.

    TAKE ONE PANEL BEHIND
    YOUR HEAD.

BRING ALL ENDS OF THE SCARF **DOWN**
    THROUGH THE LOOP OF THE SCARF CLIP.

    SPREAD OUT THE PANELS.

    CLOSE THE CLIP.

FOR AN INTERESTING VARIATION WITH FULL
HEAD COVERAGE, SEE THE DESIGN ON THE
NEXT PAGE.

FOLD A LARGE SQUARE SHAWL INTO A TRIANGLE.

DRAPE THE SHAWL ACROSS YOUR SHOULDERS AND TAKE THE SIDE PANELS TO THE BACK.

TIE A SQUARE KNOT AT THE BACK TO HOLD THE SHAWL IN PLACE.

A WAY TO WEAR YOUR SHAWL WITH THE FEELING OF CONFIDENCE.

HOW TO 'OPERATE' YOUR SCARF CLIP.

OPEN THE CLIP AND **HOLD** IT BY THE FACE OR DESIGN WITH YOUR INDEX FINGER AT THE FRONT AND YOUR THUMB AT THE BACK.   YOU CAN USE EITHER HAND,   WHICHEVER IS THE MOST COMFORTABLE FOR YOU.

FRONT

THE RING, OR LOOP, SITS ABOVE YOUR THUMB LIKE A LITTLE HALO.   JUST REMEMBER,   **DON'T** HOLD YOUR CLIP BY THE LOOP. KEEP THE LOOP CLEAR AND OPEN FOR THE SCARF TO ENTER BY HOLDING THE CLIP BY THE FACE.

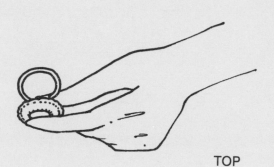

TOP

YOU WILL **ALWAYS** FEED THE SCARF **DOWN** THROUGH THE LOOP FROM THE TOP.

IT WILL BE HELPFUL IF YOU TILT THE SCARF CLIP TOWARDS YOUR BODY WHEN YOU ARE LOOKING IN THE MIRROR.

SIDE

TAKE TWO LARGE SQUARE SCARVES.

TIE TWO SQUARE KNOTS ON ANY TWO
ADJACENT CORNERS.

ADJUST THE KNOTS TO FIT YOUR
SHOULDERS.

USE A DECORATIVE BELT AT THE WAIST
TO GATHER AND ACCENT THE TUNIC.

WEAR OVER THE TOP OF A DRESS
OR A SWEATER.

A WELL MADE SCARF CLIP ACTUALLY CONTAINS THREE PARTS:

1. THE DECORATIVE FACE WHICH LOOKS LIKE A BROACH OR BUTTON.   SOME SCARF CLIPS HAVE A SOLID OR CLOSED FACE, SOME HAVE OPENINGS.   MOST SCARF DESIGNS CAN USE EITHER TYPE OF CLIP, SOME MUST USE AN OPEN FACE.

2. THE SPRING ACTION HINGE WHICH HOLDS YOUR SCARF DESIGN SECURELY.

3. THE LOOP OR RING THROUGH WHICH THE SCARF IS PASSED.   TO PREVENT DAMAGE TO YOUR SCARVES,   THIS LOOP **MUST** BE SMOOTH.

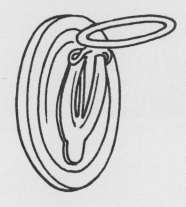

TO ACHIEVE BEAUTIFUL SCARF DESIGNS, LEARN HOW TO USE THE SCARF CLIP. THE BASIC,   SIMPLE,   EASY SECRET TO THE SCARF CLIP IS **ALL IN THE WAY YOU HOLD IT!**   LOOK AT THE PICTURES AND INSTRUCTIONS ON THE NEXT PAGE.

MATERIALS: 2 LARGE SQUARE SCARVES,
30 INCH (76 cm) OR MORE.
1/4 INCH (.5 cm) ELASTIC,
WAIST PLUS 1 INCH (2.5 cm).
SEAM BINDING.
USE A FINE NEEDLE ON MACHINE.

A. **PLACE** RIGHT SIDES OF SCARVES TOGETHER AND **STITCH** ALONG ONE SIDE LEAVING AN OPEN AREA FOR THE NECK. THIS FORMS THE SHOULDERS.
B. **CUT** A FOUR INCH (10.3 cm) SLIT FOR THE CENTRE FRONT NECK OPENING. **ROLL** THE EDGE AND HAND **STITCH.**
C. **TRY** THE SHIRT ON. **DECIDE** ON THE LOCATION OF YOUR WAIST. THEN **STITCH** ON A 1/2 INCH (1.3 cm) CASING.
D. **INSERT** ELASTIC IN THE WAIST CASING AND **SEW** THE ENDS OF THE ELASTIC TOGETHER.

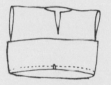

for those special occasions, we suggest you look at the designs
on pages 76, 78, 92 or 93.

INDEX (with scarf clip)